Vegetarian p·a·s·t·a

Food KIM FREEMAN
Styling CHRISTINE SHEPPARD
Photography ANDREW ELTON

A J.B. Fairfax Press Publication

INTRODUCTION

Vegetarian Pasta combines one of the world's most popular foods – pasta – with a way of eating that is becoming increasingly popular – vegetarianism. Whether it's the committed vegetarian or simply the cook looking for new and interesting ways to make the most of fresh vegetables and delicious pasta there are recipes that will appeal in this book.

Here you will discover that Italy is not the only country with a cuisine that includes pasta – many other European countries also have some wonderful pasta dishes. And, of course, there is Oriental pasta which includes Chinese egg and rice noodles and Japanese soba noodles.

No matter the flavour or the type of noodle there are recipes to suit every taste and occasion in this imaginative book.

EDITORIAL
Food Editor: Rachel Blackmore
Editor: Linda Venturoni
Editorial and Production Assistant: Heather Straton
Editorial Coordinator: Margaret Kelly
Recipe Development: Kim Freeman

Photography: Andrew Elton
Styling: Christine Sheppard

DESIGN AND PRODUCTION
Production Director: Anna Maguire
Design Manager: Drew Buckmaster
Production Editor: Sheridan Packer
Production Artist: Lulu Dougherty
Cover Design: Michele Withers

Published by J.B. Fairfax Press Pty Limited
80-82 McLachlan Avenue
Rushcutters Bay, NSW 2011, Australia
A.C.N. 003 738 430

Formatted by J.B. Fairfax Press Pty Limited
Printed by Toppan Printing Co, Singapore
PRINTED IN SINGAPORE

JBFP 357
Includes Index
ISBN 1 86343 195 0

DISTRIBUTION AND SALES
Australia: J.B. Fairfax Press Pty Limited
Ph: (02) 9361 6366 Fax: (02) 9360 6262
United Kingdom: J.B. Fairfax Press Limited
Ph: (0933) 40 2330 Fax: (0933) 40 2234

ABOUT THIS BOOK

INGREDIENTS

Unless otherwise stated the following ingredients are used in this book:

Cream — Double, suitable for whipping
Flour — White flour, plain or standard
Sugar — White sugar

WHAT'S IN A TABLESPOON?

AUSTRALIA
1 tablespoon = 20 mL or 4 teaspoons
NEW ZEALAND
1 tablespoon = 15 mL or 3 teaspoons
UNITED KINGDOM
1 tablespoon = 15 mL or 3 teaspoons
The recipes in this book were tested in Australia where a 20 mL tablespoon is standard. The tablespoon in the New Zealand and the United Kingdom sets of measuring spoons is 15 mL. For recipes using baking powder, gelatine, bicarbonate of soda, small quantities of flour and cornflour, simply add another teaspoon for each tablespoon specified.

CANNED FOODS

Can sizes vary between countries and manufacturers. You may find the quantities in this book are slightly different to what is available. Purchase and use the can size nearest to the suggested size in the recipe.

MICROWAVE IT

Where microwave instructions occur in this book, a microwave oven with a 650 watt output has been used. Wattage on domestic microwave ovens varies between 500 and 700 watts, so it may be necessary to vary cooking times slightly depending on the wattage of your oven.

CONTENTS

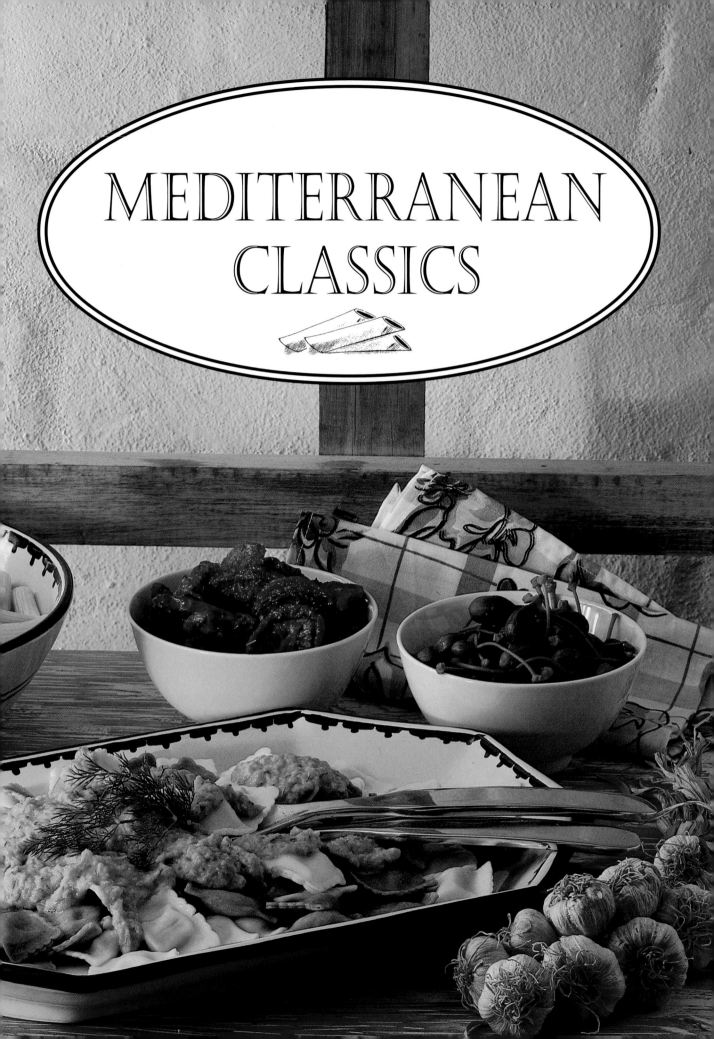

MEDITERRANEAN CLASSICS

Previous pages: Penne with Olive Pesto, Creamy Vegetable Ravioli

CREAMY VEGETABLE RAVIOLI

**750 g/1¹/₂ lb cheese and spinach ravioli
grated fresh Parmesan cheese**

CREAMY VEGETABLE SAUCE
**15 g/¹/₂ oz butter
1 leek, sliced
1 clove garlic, crushed
125 g/4 oz shelled fresh or frozen peas
2 carrots, chopped
3 cups/750 mL/1¹/₄ pt vegetable stock
¹/₃ cup/90 mL/3 fl oz cream (double)
2 tablespoons chopped fresh dill
pinch ground nutmeg
freshly ground black pepper**

1 To make sauce, melt butter in a saucepan over a medium heat, add leek and garlic and cook, stirring, for 5 minutes or until leek is soft. Add peas, carrots and stock and bring to the boil. Reduce heat and simmer for 20 minutes or until vegetables are cooked and liquid reduces. Set aside to cool slightly.

2 Place sauce mixture into a food processor or blender and process to make a purée. Return sauce to a clean saucepan and stir in cream, dill, nutmeg and black pepper to taste. Bring to simmering and simmer for 3-4 minutes or until sauce is heated.

3 Cook pasta in boiling water in a large saucepan following packet directions. Drain well and place in a serving bowl. Spoon sauce over pasta, toss to combine and scatter with Parmesan cheese.

Serves 6

Reheating pasta can be done successfully, even if it is already combined with a sauce. To reheat, place in a greased ovenproof dish, cover with aluminium foil and reheat in the oven at 180°C/350°F/Gas 4.

PENNE WITH OLIVE PESTO

**315 g/10 oz penne or other
large pasta shapes
fresh Parmesan cheese**

PESTO AND OLIVE SAUCE
**1 bunch fresh basil
60 g/2 oz pine nuts, toasted
45 g/1¹/₂ oz fresh Parmesan
cheese, chopped
2 cloves garlic, roughly chopped
¹/₂ cup/125 mL/4 fl oz olive oil
90 g/3 oz sun-dried tomatoes in oil,
drained and chopped
90 g/3 oz black olives, pitted and
chopped**

1 Cook pasta in boiling water in a large saucepan following packet directions. Drain, set aside and keep warm.

2 To make sauce, place basil leaves, pine nuts, chopped Parmesan cheese and garlic in a food processor or blender and process to finely chop. With machine running, slowly add oil and process to make a smooth paste. Stir in sun-dried tomatoes and olives.

3 To serve, spoon sauce over pasta, toss to combine and scatter with shavings of Parmesan cheese.

Serves 4

Parmesan cheese shavings make an elegant garnish for many pasta dishes. To make shavings, use a vegetable peeler or a coarse grater to remove shavings from a piece of fresh Parmesan cheese.

Stuffed Eggplant (Aubergines)

75 g/2¹/₂ oz tiny dried pasta shapes
2 large eggplant (aubergines)
salt
¹/₄ cup/60 mL/2 fl oz olive oil
1 red onion, chopped
1 clove garlic, crushed
1 teaspoon seeded, chopped
fresh red chilli
¹/₄ cup/60 mL/2 fl oz vegetable stock
60 g/2 oz black olives, pitted
and chopped
2 tablespoons chopped fresh basil
2 tablespoons chopped fresh parsley
1 tablespoon chopped fresh oregano
1 tablespoon tomato paste (purée)
60 g/2 oz grated fresh Parmesan cheese
125 g/4 oz grated mozzarella cheese

1   Cook pasta in boiling water in a large saucepan following packet directions. Drain and rinse under cold running water. Drain again and set aside.

2   Trim eggplant (aubergines) and cut in half lengthwise. Scoop out flesh leaving 5 mm/¹/₄ in thick shells. Dice eggplant (aubergine) flesh and place in a colander. Sprinkle with salt and set aside to drain for 30 minutes. Rinse under cold running water, drain and pat dry with absorbent kitchen paper.

3   Heat 2 tablespoons oil in a frying pan over a medium heat, add eggplant (aubergine) flesh and cook, stirring, for 5 minutes or until golden. Remove from pan and drain on absorbent kitchen paper.

4   Heat remaining oil in pan, add onion, garlic and chilli and cook, stirring occasionally, for 5 minutes or until onion softens slightly. Stir in eggplant (aubergine) and stock, bring to simmering and simmer for 10 minutes.

Add olives, basil, parsley, oregano and tomato paste (purée) and simmer for 2 minutes. Remove pan from the heat, add Parmesan cheese and pasta and mix to combine.

5   Divide mixture evenly between eggplant (aubergine) shells and place in a lightly greased baking dish. Cover with aluminium foil and bake for 35 minutes. Remove foil, sprinkle with mozzarella cheese and bake for 15 minutes longer or until eggplant (aubergines) are cooked and top is golden.

Serves 4

Oven temperature
180°C, 350°F, Gas 4

Any one of a range of pastina, or 'tiny pasta', recommended for this filling — among them, risoni or orzo (rice shapes), ditalini (short tubes), anellini (tiny rings) or conchigliette (tiny shells).

Stuffed Eggplant (Aubergines)

CANNELLONI WITH SPINACH SAUCE

Oven temperature
180°C, 350°F, Gas 4

125 g/4 oz instant (no precooking required) cannelloni tubes
185 g/6 oz grated mozzarella cheese

FETA AND WALNUT FILLING
185 g/6 oz feta cheese, crumbled
250 g/8 oz ricotta cheese, drained
60 g/2 oz walnuts, chopped
4 spring onions, sliced
2 tablespoons chopped fresh parsley
2 tablespoons chopped fresh mint
1 teaspoon finely grated lemon rind
1 egg, lightly beaten
1 tablespoon lemon juice
freshly ground black pepper

TOMATO AND SPINACH SAUCE
15 g/^{1}/$_2$ oz butter
1 onion, chopped
1 clove garlic, crushed
440 g/14 oz canned tomatoes, undrained and mashed
1 cup/250 mL/8 fl oz vegetable stock
1 bunch/500 g/1 lb English spinach, leaves shredded

1 To make filling, place feta cheese, ricotta cheese, walnuts, spring onions, parsley, mint, lemon rind, egg, lemon juice and black pepper to taste in a bowl and mix to combine.

2 Spoon filling into cannelloni tubes and place tubes, side by side, in a lightly greased ovenproof dish. Set aside.

3 To make sauce, melt butter in a frying pan over a medium heat, add onion and garlic and cook, stirring, for 5 minutes or until onion softens slightly. Stir in tomatoes, stock and spinach, bring to simmering and simmer for 15 minutes.

4 Spoon sauce over cannelloni tubes, cover dish with a lid or aluminium foil and bake for 25 minutes. Remove cover, sprinkle with mozzarella cheese and bake for 10-15 minutes longer or until top is golden.

Serves 4

Fresh or dried lasagne sheets may be used instead of the cannelloni tubes. Before using lasagne sheets blanch them briefly in boiling water until pliable, then cut into 13 x 16 cm/5 x 6^1/$_2$ in rectangles before filling.

Cannelloni with Spinach Sauce

ORECCHIETTE WITH VEGETABLES

315 g/10 oz dried orecchiette pasta
315 g/10 oz small broccoli florets
250 g/8 oz small cauliflower florets
125 g/4 oz butter
30 g/1 oz pine nuts
30 g/1 oz slivered almonds
3 tablespoons chopped fresh parsley
3 cloves garlic, crushed
1 fresh red chilli, seeded and diced
$^1/_4$ cup/15 g/$^1/_2$ oz coarse breadcrumbs, made from stale bread

Orecchiette means 'little ears' and this is exactly what this pasta looks like. It is made without eggs and tends to have a chewier and firmer texture than other pastas. Traditionally a homemade pasta, it can now be purchased dried from Italian food stores and some supermarkets.

1 Cook pasta in boiling water in a large saucepan following packet directions. Drain, set aside and keep warm.

2 Boil, steam or microwave broccoli and cauliflower until broccoli just changes colour. Drain, set aside and keep warm.

3 Melt butter in a frying pan over a medium heat, add pine nuts, almonds, parsley, garlic and chilli and cook, stirring, for 2 minutes or until nuts are golden. Add cauliflower and broccoli and toss well to coat with butter mixture. Add breadcrumbs and mix quickly to combine. Spoon vegetable mixture over pasta and toss to combine. Serve immediately.

Serves 6

Left: Orecchiette with Vegetables
Above: Pasta with Tomato and Basil

PASTA WITH TOMATO AND BASIL

315 g/10 oz spiral pasta
2 tablespoons chopped fresh parsley

TOMATO BASIL SAUCE
15 g/^{1}/$_2$ oz butter
1 tablespoon olive oil
1 onion, chopped
125 g/4 oz button mushrooms, sliced
2 x 440 g/14 oz canned tomatoes,
undrained and mashed
1 tablespoon chopped fresh basil
freshly ground black pepper

1   Cook pasta in boiling water in a large saucepan following packet directions. Drain, set aside and keep warm.

2   To make sauce, heat butter and oil in a frying pan over a medium heat, add onion and mushrooms and cook, stirring occasionally, for 5 minutes or until onion is soft. Add tomatoes, basil and black pepper to taste, bring to simmering and simmer, stirring occasionally, for 15 minutes or until sauce reduces and thickens.

3   To serve, spoon sauce over pasta and sprinkle with parsley.

Serves 4

VEGETARIAN LASAGNE

Oven temperature
180°C, 350°F, Gas 4

200 g/6¹/2 oz fresh lasagne sheets
185 g/6 oz grated tasty cheese
(mature Cheddar)

TOMATO SAUCE
1 tablespoon olive oil
185 g/6 oz button mushrooms, sliced
1 onion, chopped
1 clove garlic, crushed
1 teaspoon seeded, chopped
fresh red chilli
3 zucchini (courgettes), sliced
2 x 440 g/14 oz canned tomatoes,
undrained and mashed
¹/2 cup/125 mL/4 fl oz white wine
2 tablespoons chopped fresh basil
2 tablespoons chopped fresh parsley

SPINACH AND RICOTTA SAUCE
250 g/8 oz frozen spinach, thawed
and well drained
250 g/8 oz ricotta cheese, drained
1 egg, lightly beaten
freshly ground black pepper

WHITE SAUCE
60 g/2 oz butter
¹/4 cup/30 g/1 oz flour
2 cups/500 mL/16 fl oz milk
ground white pepper

1 To make Tomato Sauce, heat oil in a frying pan over a medium heat, add mushrooms, onion, garlic and chilli and cook, stirring, for 5 minutes or until onion softens slightly. Stir in zucchini (courgettes), tomatoes and wine and bring to the boil. Reduce heat and simmer for 15 minutes. Stir in basil and parsley and set aside.

2 To make Spinach and Ricotta Sauce, place spinach, ricotta cheese, egg and black pepper to taste in a bowl and mix to combine. Set aside.

3 To make White Sauce, melt butter in a saucepan over a medium heat, stir in flour and cook, stirring for 1 minute. Remove pan from heat and whisk in milk. Return pan to heat and cook, stirring, for 5 minutes or until sauce boils and thickens. Season to taste with white pepper.

4 To assemble, line base of a lightly greased ovenproof dish with one-third of the lasagne sheets, cutting to size as necessary. Top with half the Tomato Sauce, then half the remaining lasagne sheets, the remaining Tomato Sauce and remaining lasagne sheets.

5 Spread Spinach and Ricotta Sauce over lasagne, pour over White Sauce and sprinkle with tasty cheese (mature Cheddar). Bake for 30-40 minutes or until mixture is hot and bubbling and top golden.

Serves 6

For easier serving, allow lasagne to stand in a warm place for 20-30 minutes to settle before cutting.

Above: Mushroom and Pasta
Soup
Right: Pasta with Artichoke Sauce

MUSHROOM AND PASTA SOUP

Use dried Italian porcini mushrooms for authenticity, although any Oriental dried mushroom such as shiitake or clouds ears may be used to help intensify the flavour of this soup. Angel's hair pasta, known as *capelli d'angelo*, is an extremely long thin pasta purchased fresh or dried in coils to prevent it from breaking. If unavailable, substitute with very thin dried spaghetti or vermicelli.

30 g/1 oz dried mushrooms
5 cups/1.2 litres/2 pt hot water
30 g/1 oz fresh button mushrooms,
sliced
1 carrot, cut into thin strips
1 stalk celery, cut into thin strips
4 spring onions, cut into thin strips
$^{1}/_{2}$ cup/125 mL/4 fl oz dry sherry
125 g/4 oz fresh angel's hair pasta
3 tablespoons chopped fresh parsley
freshly ground black pepper

1   Place dried mushrooms in a large bowl, pour over hot water and set aside to stand for 20-30 minutes or until mushrooms are tender. Drain and place liquid in a saucepan. Cut soaked mushrooms into thin strips.

2   Add soaked mushrooms, fresh mushrooms, carrot, celery, spring onions, sherry and pasta to pan and bring to the boil. Reduce heat and simmer for 5 minutes or until pasta is cooked. Stir in parsley and season to taste with black pepper.

Serves 6

16

PASTA WITH ARTICHOKE SAUCE

375 g/12 oz fresh fettuccine

ARTICHOKE AND LEEK SAUCE
30 g/1 oz butter
1 leek, sliced
1 clove garlic, crushed
$^1/_4$ cup/60 mL/2 fl oz dry white wine
1$^1/_4$ cups/315 mL/10 fl oz cream
(double)
3 teaspoons tomato paste (purée)
440 g/14 oz canned artichoke hearts,
drained and sliced
2 tablespoons chopped fresh basil
freshly ground black pepper

1 Cook pasta in boiling water in a large saucepan following packet directions. Drain, set aside and keep warm.

2 To make sauce, melt butter in a frying pan over a low heat, add leek and garlic and cook, stirring, for 5 minutes or until leek is soft. Stir in wine, bring to simmering and simmer for 5 minutes.

3 Stir in cream and tomato paste (purée), bring to simmering and simmer for 2 minutes. Add artichoke hearts, basil and black pepper to taste and cook for 2-3 minutes longer or until hot. Spoon sauce over pasta and toss to combine.

Serves 4

For variety and visual interest, purchase an assortment of plain, green (spinach) and red (tomato) fettuccine.

PENNE WITH CHILLI AND TOMATO

1 large eggplant (aubergine), cut
into 1 cm/^{1}/$_2$ in cubes
salt
315 g/10 oz penne
^{1}/$_4$ cup/60 mL/2 fl oz olive oil
1 onion, sliced
1 red pepper, chopped
2 fresh red chillies, seeded and diced
2 cloves garlic, crushed
625 g/1^1/$_4$ lb ripe tomatoes, peeled
seeded and chopped
^{1}/$_4$ cup/60 mL/2 fl oz water
1 tablespoon tomato paste (purée)
3 tablespoons chopped fresh parsley

For a complete meal, serve
this robust dish with a tossed
green salad and crusty
bread and finish with a
selection of fresh fruit.

1 Place eggplant (aubergine) in a
colander, sprinkle with salt and set
aside to drain for 30 minutes. Rinse
eggplant (aubergine) under cold
running water and pat dry with
absorbent kitchen paper.

2 Cook pasta in boiling water in a large
saucepan following packet directions.
Drain, set aside and keep warm.

3 Heat 2 tablespoons oil in a frying
pan over a medium heat, add eggplant
(aubergine) and cook, stirring, for
5 minutes. Remove from pan and
drain on absorbent kitchen paper.

4 Heat remaining oil in pan, add
onion, red pepper, chillies and garlic
and cook, stirring, for 5 minutes or until
onion softens. Stir in tomatoes, water,
tomato paste (purée) and eggplant
(aubergine), bring to simmering and
simmer for 10 minutes. Spoon sauce
over pasta and sprinkle with parsley.

Serves 4

SPINACH MACARONI CHEESE

Oven temperature
180°C, 350°F, Gas 4

500 g/1 lb pasta shells
^{1}/$_2$ bunch/250 g/8 oz English spinach,
leaves shredded

CHEESE SAUCE
60 g/2 oz butter
2 tablespoons flour
2^1/$_2$ cups/600 mL/1 pt milk
100 g/3^1/$_2$ oz grated Gruyère cheese
75 g/2^1/$_2$ oz grated tasty cheese
(mature Cheddar)
freshly ground black pepper

PARMESAN TOPPING
1 cup/125 g/4 oz dried breadcrumbs
60 g/2 oz butter, melted
45 g/1^1/$_2$ oz grated fresh Parmesan cheese

A combination of three
cheeses – Gruyère, tasty
(mature Cheddar) and
fresh Parmesan – provide
body and a robust flavour
to simple macaroni cheese.
This is an excellent way to
use up small pieces of any
assorted cheeses leftover
after a dinner party.

1 Cook pasta in boiling water in a large
saucepan following packet directions.
Drain, place in a greased ovenproof
dish and set aside.

2 Boil, steam or microwave spinach
until just wilted. Drain well, add to
pasta and toss to combine.

3 To make sauce, melt butter in a
saucepan over a medium heat, stir in
flour and cook, stirring, for 1 minute.
Remove pan from heat, whisk in milk,
then cook, stirring, for 5 minutes or
until sauce boils and thickens. Stir in
Gruyère cheese, tasty cheese (mature
Cheddar) and black pepper to taste.
Pour over pasta and mix to combine.

4 To make topping, combine
breadcrumbs, butter and Parmesan
cheese and sprinkle over pasta. Bake
for 20-30 minutes or until sauce is hot
and bubbling and top is golden.

Serves 6

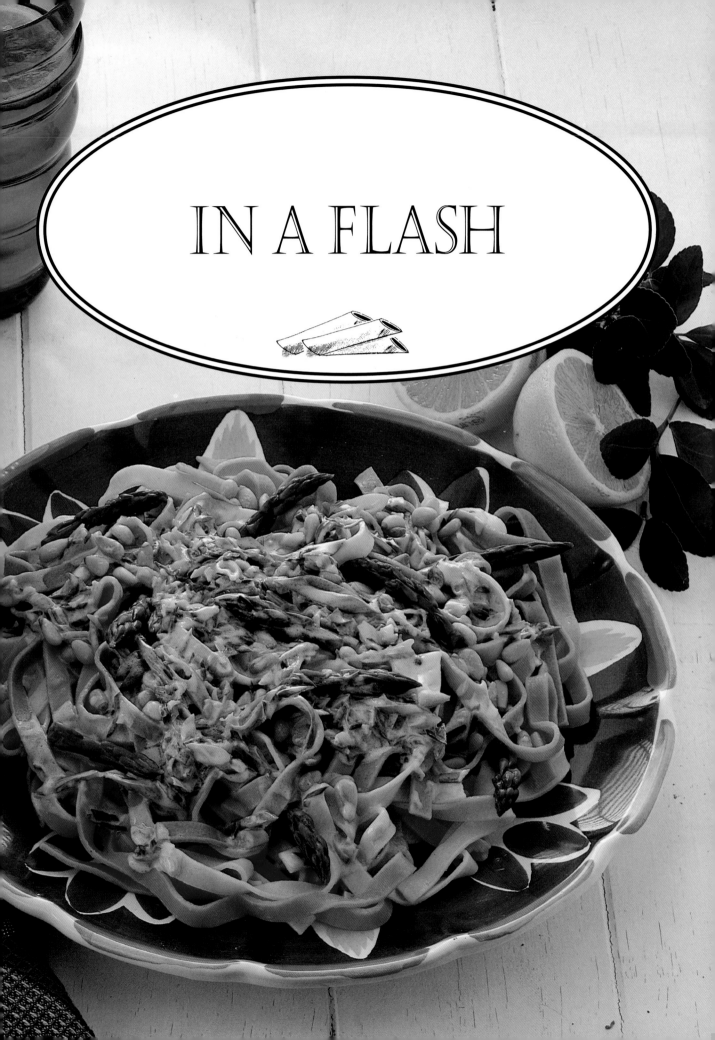

IN A FLASH

Previous pages: Farfalle with Whisky Sauce, Creamy Asparagus Fettuccine

FARFALLE WITH WHISKY SAUCE

375 g/12 oz farfalle

WHISKY AND PEPPERCORN SAUCE
15 g/^{1}/$_{2}$ oz butter
125 g/4 oz button mushrooms, sliced
4 spring onions, sliced
1^{1}/$_{4}$ cups/315 g/10 oz sour cream
2 teaspoons French mustard
2 teaspoons crushed green
peppercorns
^{1}/$_{4}$ cup/60 mL/2 fl oz vegetable stock
1 tablespoon whisky

1 Cook pasta in boiling water in a large saucepan following packet directions. Drain, set aside and keep warm.

2 To make sauce, melt butter in a frying pan over a medium heat, add mushrooms and spring onions and cook, stirring, for 2-3 minutes or until mushrooms are soft.

3 Stir in sour cream, mustard, peppercorns, stock and whisky, bring to simmering and simmer for 1 minute. Spoon sauce over pasta and toss gently to combine.

Serves 4

Farfalle means butterflies and this is what this pretty bow-shaped pasta looks like.

CREAMY ASPARAGUS FETTUCCINE

500 g/1 lb fresh fettuccine

CREAMY ASPARAGUS SAUCE
15 g/^{1}/$_{2}$ oz butter
6 spring onions, sliced
1 clove garlic, crushed
2 cups/500 mL/16 fl oz cream (double)
375 g/12 oz asparagus, blanched and cut into 2.5 cm/1 in pieces
60 g/2 oz pine nuts, toasted
freshly ground black pepper

1 Cook pasta in boiling water in a large saucepan following packet directions. Drain, set aside and keep warm.

2 To make sauce, melt butter in a saucepan over a medium heat, add spring onions and garlic and cook, stirring, for 2 minutes or until onions are soft.

3 Stir in cream, bring to simmering and simmer for 3 minutes. Stir in asparagus and cook for 2 minutes longer. Add pine nuts and black pepper to taste. Spoon sauce over pasta and toss to combine. Serve immediately.

Serves 4

Fresh or packaged dried pasta? Which is the best? Neither is superior — they are just different. Fresh pasta is more delicate and keeps for only a few days, while dried pasta is more stable and ideal for serving with heartier sauces and to have on hand as a store cupboard ingredient.

MEDITERRANEAN PASTA

375 g/12 oz pasta shells

TOMATO AND PEPPER SAUCE
**1 tablespoon olive oil
1 onion, sliced
1 clove garlic, crushed
$^1/_2$ red pepper, cut into strips
$^1/_2$ green pepper, cut into strips
$^1/_2$ large bulb fennel, sliced
2 x 440 g/14 oz canned tomatoes,
undrained and mashed
$^1/_2$ cup/125 mL/4 fl oz water
2 tablespoons tomato paste (purée)
2 teaspoons balsamic vinegar
1 teaspoon dried oregano leaves
freshly ground black pepper**

1 Cook pasta in boiling water in a large saucepan following packet directions. Drain, set aside and keep warm.

2 To make sauce, heat oil in a saucepan over a medium heat, add onion and garlic and cook, stirring, for 3 minutes or until onion softens slightly. Add red and green peppers and fennel and cook, stirring, for 2 minutes longer. Stir in tomatoes, water, tomato paste (purée), vinegar and oregano, bring to simmering and simmer for 5 minutes. Season to taste with black pepper. Spoon sauce over pasta and serve.

Serves 4

The anise flavour of fennel is delicious in this hearty sauce. When fresh fennel is unavailable, substitute with 1 teaspoon fennel seeds, lightly crushing them in the palm of your hand before cooking with the onion.

CRISPY NOODLES AND VEGETABLES

315 g/10 oz fresh thin egg noodles
vegetable oil for deep-frying
500 g/1 lb packaged frozen Chinese
stir-fry mixed vegetables

PEANUT SAUCE
$^3/_4$ cup/200 g/6$^1/_2$ oz crunchy
peanut butter
1 tablespoon brown sugar
1 clove garlic, crushed
1$^1/_2$ cups/375 mL/12 fl oz coconut milk
2 tablespoons light soy sauce
2 teaspoons hot chilli sauce

1 Cook noodles in boiling water in a large saucepan for 2-3 minutes, drain and dry on absorbent kitchen paper. Heat oil in a large saucepan over a medium heat until a cube of bread dropped in browns in 50 seconds. Deep-fry noodles, in batches, for 2-3 minutes or until puffed and crispy. Drain on absorbent kitchen paper, set aside and keep warm.

2 Cook mixed vegetables following packet directions. Drain, set aside and keep warm.

3 To make sauce, place peanut butter, sugar, garlic, coconut milk, soy sauce and chilli sauce in a saucepan and cook over a low heat, stirring, for 3-5 minutes or until hot. To serve, divide noodles between serving plates, top with vegetables and sauce.

Serves 4

Any thin spaghetti type noodle can be used in place of the egg noodles in this recipe. You might like to try spaghetti, linguini or fettuccine.

NOODLES WITH BOK CHOY SAUCE

250 g/8 oz quick-cooking noodles

BOK CHOY SAUCE
1 tablespoon vegetable oil
2 bunches/500 g/1 lb baby bok choy,
leaves separated and trimmed
$^1/_3$ cup/90 mL/3 fl oz soy sauce
2 tablespoons sesame oil
2 tablespoons kechap manis
2 tablespoons sweet chilli sauce
2 tablespoons pickled ginger
315 g/10 oz tofu, cut into
1 cm/$^1/_2$ in cubes
155 g/5 oz bean sprouts

1 Cook noodles in boiling water in a large saucepan following packet directions. Drain, set aside and keep warm.

2 To make sauce, heat oil in a wok or frying pan over a high heat, add bok choy and stir-fry for 2-3 minutes. Add soy sauce, sesame oil, kechap manis, chilli sauce and ginger, bring to simmering and simmer for 1 minute.

3 Add tofu and bean sprouts and stir-fry for 2-3 minutes or until heated through. Add noodles to pan and toss to combine. Serve immediately.

Serves 4

Noodles with Boy Choy Sauce,
Crispy Noodles and Vegetables

Kechap manis, sometimes called sweet soy sauce or Indonesian soy sauce is a thick sweet seasoning sauce, made of soy sauce, sugar and spices. If unavailable soy sauce or a mixture of soy sauce and dark corn syrup or golden syrup can be used in its place.

FETTUCCINE WITH CORN SAUCE

500 g/1 lb fresh fettuccine

CORN AND CORIANDER SAUCE
1 tablespoon olive oil
1 red pepper, chopped
440 g/14 oz canned creamed sweet corn
$^1/4$ cup/60 mL/2 fl oz water
2 teaspoons hot chilli sauce
2 tablespoons chopped fresh coriander
freshly ground black pepper

1   Cook pasta in boiling water in a large saucepan following packet directions. Drain, set aside and keep warm.

2   To make sauce, heat oil in a saucepan over a medium heat, add red pepper and cook, stirring, for 2 minutes or until pepper is soft. Stir in sweet corn, water, chilli sauce, coriander and black pepper to taste and cook for 2 minutes longer or until sauce is hot. Spoon sauce over pasta and toss to combine.

Serves 4

Creamed sweet corn, chilli sauce and fresh coriander combine to provide unusual but delightful flavours.

RAVIOLI WITH LEMON SAUCE

Left: Fettuccine with Corn Sauce
Above: Ravioli with Lemon Sauce

500 g/1 lb cheese and spinach ravioli
30 g/1 oz slivered almonds, toasted

LEMON CREAM SAUCE
30 g/1 oz butter
1 clove garlic, crushed
1¼ cups/315 mL/10 fl oz cream
(double)
¼ cup/60 mL/2 fl oz lemon juice
30 g/1 oz grated fresh Parmesan cheese
3 tablespoons snipped fresh chives
1 teaspoon finely grated lemon rind
2 tablespoons chopped fresh parsley
freshly ground black pepper

1 Cook pasta in boiling water in a large saucepan following packet directions. Drain, set aside and keep warm.

2 To make sauce, melt butter in a frying pan over a low heat, add garlic and cook, stirring, for 1 minute. Stir in cream, lemon juice, Parmesan cheese, chives and lemon rind, bring to simmering and simmer for 2 minutes. Add parsley and black pepper to taste and cook for 1 minute longer. Spoon sauce over pasta and toss to combine. Scatter with almonds and serve.

Serves 4

Equally delicious made with cheese and spinach agnolotti (crescent or half-moon shaped ravioli) or tortellini.

Olive and Feta Penne

315 g/10 oz penne
1 tablespoon sesame seeds, toasted

OLIVE AND FETA SAUCE
3 tablespoons olive oil
1 clove garlic, crushed
2 large yellow zucchini (courgettes),
peeled into long strips
2 large green zucchini (courgettes),
peeled into long strips
125 g/4 oz feta cheese, crumbled
1 tablespoon olive pâté (paste)
freshly ground black pepper

1 Cook pasta in boiling water in a large saucepan following packet directions. Drain, set aside and keep warm.

2 To make sauce, heat 1 tablespoon oil in a frying pan over a medium heat, add garlic and yellow and green zucchini (courgettes) and cook, stirring, for 2 minutes or until zucchini (courgettes) soften slightly. Add feta cheese, olive pâté (paste) and remaining oil, mix to combine and heat for 2-3 minutes. Season to taste with black pepper. Spoon sauce over pasta, toss to combine and sprinkle with sesame seeds.

Serves 4

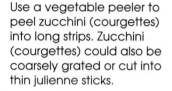

Use a vegetable peeler to peel zucchini (courgettes) into long strips. Zucchini (courgettes) could also be coarsely grated or cut into thin julienne sticks.

Pasta with Spinach Mint Sauce

500 g/1 lb fresh or dried spaghetti
or bucatini

SPINACH AND MINT SAUCE
500 g/1 lb frozen spinach, thawed
and drained
250 g/8 oz feta cheese, crumbled
1 cup/200 g/6^1/2 oz natural yogurt
3 tablespoons chopped fresh mint
1 teaspoon finely grated lemon rind

1 Cook pasta in boiling water in a large saucepan following packet directions. Drain, set aside and keep warm.

2 To make sauce, place spinach, feta cheese, yogurt, mint and lemon rind in the pan in which the pasta was cooked and cook over a low heat, stirring, for 2 minutes or until heated through.

3 Return pasta to pan and toss to combine. Cook over a low heat, stirring, for 2 minutes longer or until mixture is hot. Serve immediately.

Serves 4

Bucatini is hollow spaghetti. A combination of any chopped fresh herbs of your choice may be used instead of the mint.

*Pasta with Spinach Mint Sauce,
Olive and Feta Penne*

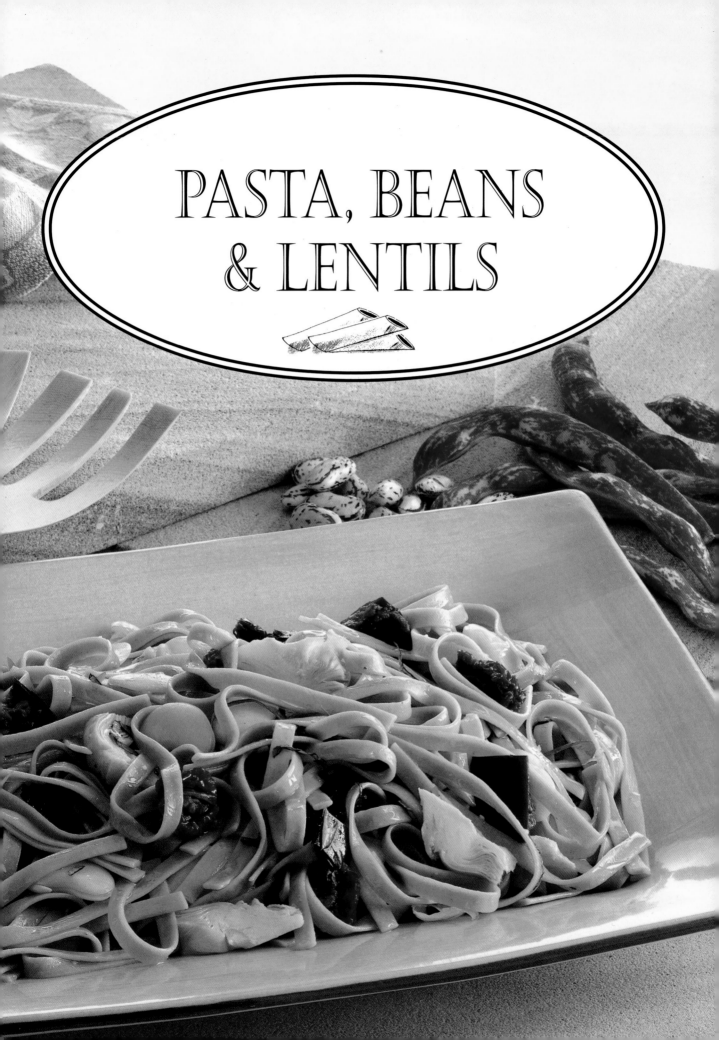

PASTA, BEANS & LENTILS

FETTUCCINE AND LIMA SALAD

Previous pages: Spinach and Borlotti Salad, Fettuccine and Lima Salad

155 g/5 oz dried lima or butter beans
1 clove garlic, crushed
2 tablespoons olive oil
1 tablespoon balsamic vinegar
250 g/8 oz dried spinach fettuccine
440 g/14 oz canned artichoke hearts,
drained and chopped
155 g/5 oz marinated eggplant
(aubergines), drained and chopped
125 g/4 oz sun-dried tomatoes in oil,
drained and chopped
6 spring onions, sliced
3 tablespoons shredded fresh basil

Marinated eggplant (aubergines) are available from Italian delicatessens and some supermarkets or you can marinate them yourself. To marinate eggplant (aubergines), cut eggplant (aubergines) into slices and cook under a hot grill for 4-5 minutes each side or until cooked through. Place eggplant (aubergines) in a bowl, add crushed garlic and sprinkle with olive oil and balsamic or red wine vinegar, toss and marinate for several hours.

1   Place beans in a large bowl, cover with cold water and soak overnight. Drain. Place beans in a large saucepan, cover with cold water and bring to the boil. Boil for 10 minutes, then reduce heat and simmer for 1 hour or until beans are tender. Drain and place beans in a salad bowl. Add garlic, then sprinkle with oil and vinegar and toss to combine. Cover and marinate in the refrigerator for 2 hours.

2   Cook pasta in boiling water in a large saucepan following packet directions. Drain and rinse under cold running water. Drain again and set aside.

3   Add pasta, artichoke hearts, eggplant (aubergines), sun-dried tomatoes, spring onions and basil to beans and toss to combine.

Serves 6

SPINACH AND BORLOTTI SALAD

185 g/6 oz dried borlotti beans
250 g/8 oz penne or other tubular pasta
1 bunch/500 g/1 lb English spinach,
leaves torn into bite-sized pieces
155 g/5 oz cherry tomatoes, halved
1 red onion, sliced

HERB AND LEMON DRESSING
2 tablespoons chopped fresh parsley
1 tablespoon chopped fresh basil
1 teaspoon finely grated lemon rind
1 clove garlic, crushed
$^1/_2$ cup/125 mL/4 fl oz olive oil
2 tablespoons lemon juice
freshly ground black pepper

An assortment of fresh salad greens can be used in place of the spinach. For a complete meal finish with a fresh fruit platter served with a yogurt dip.

1   Place beans in a large bowl, cover with cold water and soak overnight. Drain. Place beans in a large saucepan, cover with cold water and bring to the boil. Boil for 10 minutes, then reduce heat and simmer for 1-$1^1/_2$ hours or until beans are tender. Drain, place beans in a salad bowl and cool.

2   Cook pasta in boiling water in a large saucepan following packet directions. Drain, rinse under cold running water and drain again.

3   Add pasta, spinach, tomatoes and onion to beans and toss to combine.

4   To make dressing, place parsley, basil, lemon rind, garlic, oil, lemon juice and black pepper to taste in a small bowl and whisk to combine. Spoon dressing over salad and toss to combine. Cover and chill for 1 hour before serving.

Serves 6-8

STUFFED VINE LEAVES

250 g/8 oz preserved vine leaves
1 tablespoon olive oil
1 onion, chopped
1 clove garlic, crushed
90 g/3 oz risoni or orzo pasta
(small rice shapes)
185 g/6 oz ripe tomatoes, peeled
and chopped
155 g/5 oz canned sweet corn and red
pepper mix, drained
155 g/5 oz canned lima beans, rinsed
and drained
2 tablespoons dried currants
2 tablespoons chopped fresh parsley
1 tablespoon chopped fresh mint
pinch ground cinnamon
2 cups/500 mL/16 fl oz vegetable
stock

1   Soak vine leaves in cold water for 20 minutes, then drain and blanch in boiling water for 3 minutes. Drain well, then rinse under cold running water and set aside.

2   Heat oil in a frying pan over a medium heat, add onion and garlic and cook, stirring, for 5 minutes or until onion softens slightly. Add pasta and tomatoes and cook over a low heat, stirring, for 3 minutes. Stir in sweet corn and red pepper mix, lima beans, currants, parsley, mint and cinnamon. Remove pan from heat and set aside.

3   Place each vine leaf, shiny side down, on the work surface. Place a teaspoon of pasta mixture in the centre of each leaf, fold stem end over filling, then fold in sides and roll up. Gently squeeze rolls in palm of your hand.

4   Line a large saucepan with some of the imperfect vine leaves. Pack rolls tightly together, seam-side down, in saucepan and pour over stock. Place a plate on top of rolls to weigh down. Cover pan, bring to simmering and simmer for 30 minutes or until cooked.

Makes approximately 40

Vine leaves are available at health food shops and delicatessens. A mix of canned sweet corn, lima beans and red pepper is sometimes available and can be used.
Serve rolls accompanied by feta cheese, marinated olives, lemon wedges and a bowl of natural yogurt for dipping.

Stuffed Vine Leaves

TOMATO AND CHICKPEA SOUP

1 tablespoon olive oil
1 onion, sliced
2 cloves garlic, crushed
155 g/5 oz spiral pasta
1 carrot, chopped
1 zucchini (courgette), sliced
440 g/14 oz canned tomatoes,
undrained and roughly chopped
$1/2$ teaspoon dried oregano leaves
$1/2$ teaspoon dried basil leaves
8 cups/2 litres/$3^1/2$ pt vegetable stock
440 g/14 oz canned chickpeas,
rinsed and drained

If canned chickpeas are unavailable, use cold cooked chickpeas instead. To cook chickpeas, soak overnight in cold water. Drain. Place in a large saucepan, cover with cold water and bring to the boil over a medium heat. Reduce heat and simmer for 45-60 minutes or until tender. Drain and cool.

1 Heat oil in a large saucepan over a low heat, add onion and garlic and cook, stirring, for 5 minutes or until onion softens slightly. Add pasta, carrot, zucchini (courgette), tomatoes, oregano, basil and stock.

2 Bring to the boil, then reduce heat and simmer for 10 minutes. Stir in chickpeas and cook for 5-10 minutes longer or until pasta is cooked.

Serves 6

GREEN LENTIL AND PEA SOUP

500 g/1 lb shelled fresh or frozen peas
75 g/$2^1/2$ oz green lentils
1 onion, finely chopped
4 cups/1 litre/$1^3/4$ pt vegetable stock
60 g/2 oz butter
$1/4$ cup/30 g/1 oz flour
2 teaspoons hot Madras curry powder
4 cups/1 litre/$1^3/4$ pt water
125 g/4 oz thin spaghetti, broken
into pieces
$1/2$ cup/125 mL/4 fl oz cream (single)
2 tablespoons chopped fresh mint
freshly ground black pepper

Cheese Toasts are delicious served with this soup. To make Cheese Toasts, cut 1 small French stick into 5 mm/$^1/4$ in thick slices and toast on one side under a preheated medium grill until golden. Combine 100 g/ $3^1/2$ oz cream cheese, 45 g/ $1^1/2$ oz grated Parmesan cheese, 45 g/$1^1/2$ oz grated Gruyère cheese and 1 teaspoon crushed black peppercorns. Spread cheese mixture over untoasted sides of bread. Return to grill and cook for 3-4 minutes longer or until cheese melts.

1 Place peas, lentils, onion and stock in a saucepan and bring to the boil. Reduce heat and simmer, stirring occasionally, for 40-45 minutes or until lentils are cooked. Remove pan from heat and set aside to cool slightly.

2 Purée pea mixture in batches in a food processor or blender. Set aside.

3 Melt butter in a saucepan over a low heat, add flour and curry powder and cook, stirring, for 1 minute. Remove pan from heat, gradually stir in the water and continue mixing until smooth. Return pan to heat and cook, stirring, until soup boils and thickens. Reduce heat, stir in pea purée and spaghetti and simmer for 10 minutes or until spaghetti is cooked. Stir in cream, mint and black pepper to taste, bring to simmering and simmer for 1 minute.

Serves 6

*Tomato and Chickpea Soup,
Green Lentil and Pea Soup*

CURRY VEGETABLE PANCAKES

1 tablespoon vegetable oil
1 leek, cut into thin strips
1 carrot, cut into thin strips
250 g/8 oz broccoli florets
315 g/10 oz canned butter beans,
rinsed and drained

PASTA AND POLENTA PANCAKES
75 g/2^1/$_2$ oz tiny dried pasta shapes,
such as risoni or orzo, anellini,
ditalini or conchigliette)
^{1}/$_2$ cup/90 g/3 oz cornmeal (polenta)
^{3}/$_4$ cup/185 mL/6 fl oz boiling water
^{1}/$_2$ cup/125 mL/4 fl oz milk
1 egg, lightly beaten
^{3}/$_4$ cup/90 g/3 oz flour
butter

COCONUT CURRY SAUCE
15 g/^{1}/$_2$ oz butter
1 tablespoon curry powder or
curry paste
1 teaspoon finely grated fresh ginger
^{1}/$_4$ teaspoon ground turmeric
1^1/$_2$ cups/375 mL/12 fl oz coconut
cream
1 tablespoon chopped fresh coriander

1 To make pancakes, cook pasta in boiling water in a large saucepan following packet directions. Drain and rinse under cold running water. Drain again and set aside. Place cornmeal (polenta) in a large bowl and stir in boiling water. Cover and set aside for 15 minutes.

2 Add milk, egg, flour and pasta to cornmeal mixture and mix well to combine. Melt a little butter in a frying pan over a low heat and when butter starts to foam, pour ^{1}/$_4$ cup/60 mL/ 2 fl oz batter into pan and cook for 2 minutes or until golden, turn over and cook for 2 minutes longer. Remove pancake, set aside and keep warm. Repeat with remaining batter.

3 To make sauce, heat butter in a frying pan over a medium heat, add curry powder or paste, ginger and turmeric and cook, stirring, for 2 minutes. Stir in coconut cream and coriander, bring to simmering and simmer for 1-2 minutes.

4 Heat oil in a wok or frying pan over a medium heat, add leek and stir-fry for 1-2 minutes or until just tender. Add carrot and broccoli and stir-fry for 4-5 minutes longer or until vegetables are just tender. Add beans and cook for 1-2 minutes or until heated through.

5 To assemble, place a pancake on each serving plate, top with vegetable mixture, then with a second pancake. Spoon over sauce and serve immediately.

Serves 4-6

If coconut cream is unavailable, substitute with coconut milk. Although coconut cream is thicker than coconut milk, they are interchangeable in recipes. Both products can be purchased canned, as a long-life product in cartons or as a powder to which you add water. Once opened, they have a short life and should be used within a day or so.

PASTA-TOPPED RATATOUILLE

Oven temperature
180°C, 350°F, Gas 4

PASTA TOPPING
315 g/10 oz small pasta shapes
of your choice
90 g/3 oz butter, melted
45 g/1¹/₂ oz grated fresh Parmesan
cheese

BEAN RATATOUILLE
2 small eggplant (aubergines), sliced
salt
olive oil
1 large onion, thinly sliced
1 red pepper, sliced
1 green pepper, sliced
2 large zucchini (courgettes), sliced
185 g/6 oz button mushrooms, sliced
500 g/1 lb tomatoes, sliced
315 g/10 oz canned three bean mix,
rinsed and drained
1 clove garlic, crushed
1 teaspoon dried oregano leaves
1 teaspoon dried basil leaves
¹/₂ teaspoon chilli paste (sambal oelek)
440 g/14 oz canned tomatoes,
undrained and puréed
¹/₃ cup/90 mL/3 fl oz vegetable stock
freshly ground black pepper

1 To make topping, cook pasta in boiling water in a large saucepan following packet directions. Drain, rinse under cold running water and drain again. Place pasta, butter and Parmesan cheese in a bowl and mix to combine. Set aside.

2 To make ratatouille, place eggplant (aubergines) in a colander, sprinkle with salt and set aside to drain for 30 minutes. Rinse eggplant (aubergines) under cold running water and pat dry with absorbent kitchen paper.

3 Heat 2 tablespoons oil in a frying pan over a medium heat and cook eggplant (aubergines), in batches, for 3-4 minutes on each side or until soft. Drain on absorbent kitchen paper. Cook onion, red pepper, green pepper, zucchini (courgettes) and mushrooms separately in the same way, adding more oil as necessary.

4 Arrange eggplant (aubergine) slices, onion, red and green peppers, zucchini (courgettes), mushrooms and tomatoes in layers in a large ovenproof dish. Place bean mix, garlic, oregano, basil, chilli paste (sambal oelek), puréed tomatoes, stock and black pepper to taste in a large bowl and mix to combine. Pour bean mixture over vegetables and bake for 45 minutes.

5 Spoon topping over vegetables and bake for 20-30 minutes longer or until topping is golden and vegetables are tender.

Serves 8

Any small pasta shape such as fusilli (spirals or twists), farfalle (butterflies or bow ties), conchiglie (medium-size shells), dried gnocchi or small elbow (short-cut) macaroni is suitable for this recipe.
Canned three bean mix as used in this recipe is a mixture of butter beans, red kidney beans and lima beans. Any canned mixed beans are suitable to use.

Pasta-topped Ratatouille

PASTA BALLS WITH LENTIL SAUCE

125 g/4 oz fresh angel's hair pasta,
cut into small pieces
250 g/8 oz carrots, grated
$^1/_2$ cup/60 g/2 oz flour
1 teaspoon ground cumin
1 egg, lightly beaten
vegetable oil for shallow-frying

LENTIL SAUCE
30 g/1 oz butter
1 onion, chopped
1 clove garlic, crushed
1 fresh red chilli, seeded and chopped
2 teaspoons garam masala
1 teaspoon ground turmeric
200 g/6$^1/_2$ oz green lentils
6 cups/1.5 litres/2$^1/_2$ pt water
2 tablespoons tomato paste (purée)
4 tablespoons chopped fresh coriander

For quicker preparation, in step 2 cook the pasta balls in the microwave rather than the frying pan. To cook in the microwave, place six pasta balls on a microwavable plate and cook on HIGH (100%) for 40-50 seconds or until balls are just firm. If cooking in the microwave there is no need to chill the pasta balls before cooking.
If angel's hair pasta is unavailable, substitute with fresh or dried thin spaghetti or vermicelli.

1   Cook pasta in boiling water in a large saucepan following packet directions. Drain, rinse under cold running water and drain again.

2   Place pasta, carrots, flour, cumin and egg in a bowl and mix to combine. Form pasta mixture into small balls, place on a plate lined with plastic food wrap and chill for 20-30 minutes. Heat oil in a frying pan over a medium heat. Add pasta balls and cook, turning several times, for 4-5 minutes or until firm.

3   To make sauce, melt butter in a saucepan over a medium heat, add onion, garlic, chilli, garam masala and turmeric and cook, stirring, for 5 minutes or until onion is soft.

4   Stir in lentils, water and tomato paste (purée) and bring to the boil. Reduce heat and simmer, stirring occasionally, for 35-40 minutes or until lentils are cooked and sauce is thick. Stir in coriander and simmer for 2 minutes. Serve with pasta balls.

Serves 6

Left: Pasta Balls with Lentil Sauce
Right: Pasta and Lentil Loaf

PASTA AND LENTIL LOAF

75 g/2^1/$_2$ oz small pasta shapes
125 g/4 oz brown lentils
2 cups/125 g/4 oz wholemeal
breadcrumbs, made from stale bread
1 onion, grated
1 carrot, grated
2 stalks celery, chopped
60 g/2 oz pine nuts
^{1}/$_4$ cup/60 mL/2 fl oz tomato sauce
^{1}/$_4$ cup/60 mL/2 fl oz water
2 eggs, lightly beaten
2 tablespoons Worcestershire sauce
freshly ground black pepper

1   Cook pasta in boiling water in a
large saucepan following packet
directions. Drain and rinse under cold
running water. Drain again and set
aside. Wash and drain lentils.

2   Place pasta, lentils, breadcrumbs,
onion, carrot, celery, pine nuts, tomato
sauce, water, eggs, Worcestershire sauce
and black pepper to taste in a bowl and
mix to combine. Spoon mixture into a
lightly greased 11 x 21 cm/4^1/$_2$ x 8^1/$_2$ in
loaf tin and bake for 45 minutes or
until loaf is firm.

Serves 6

Oven temperature
180°C, 350°F, Gas 4

When choosing the pasta
for this loaf, refer to the tip
on page 38.

41

MUSHROOM LASAGNE ROLLS

Oven temperature
180°C, 350°F, Gas 4

Lasagne rolls are delicious served with a salad of lightly cooked mixed vegetables tossed with balsamic vinegar or Italian dressing.

2 fresh lasagne sheets
125 g/4 oz grated tasty cheese
(mature Cheddar)
30 g/1 oz walnuts, roughly chopped

MUSHROOM RICOTTA FILLING
2 tablespoons olive oil
1 onion, finely chopped
185 g/6 oz button mushrooms, finely chopped
45 g/1$^{1}/_{2}$ oz red lentils
250 g/8 oz ricotta cheese, drained
60 g/2 oz walnuts, chopped
2 tablespoons chopped fresh parsley
freshly ground black pepper

WHITE SAUCE
60 g/2 oz butter
$^{1}/_{4}$ cup/30 g/1 oz flour
2 cups/500 mL/16 fl oz milk

1 Cut each lasagne sheet into four rectangles, each measuring approximately 10 x 15 cm/4 x 6 in. Cover and set aside.

2 To make filling, heat oil in a frying pan over a medium heat, add onion and cook, stirring, for 5 minutes or until onion is soft. Add mushrooms and cook, stirring, for 2-3 minutes longer or until mushrooms are cooked. Stir in lentils, ricotta cheese, walnuts, parsley and black pepper to taste. Set aside.

3 To make sauce, melt butter in a saucepan over a low heat, add flour and cook, stirring, for 1 minute. Remove pan from heat and gradually stir in milk. Return to a medium heat, bring to simmering and simmer, stirring constantly, for 1 minute. Season to taste with black pepper.

4 To assemble, divide filling between pasta rectangles and roll up to enclose. Pour one-quarter of the sauce over the base of a lightly greased ovenproof dish. Arrange rolls, side by side, in dish, pour over remaining sauce, sprinkle with tasty cheese (mature Cheddar) and walnuts and bake for 35-40 minutes or until lasagne is cooked.

Serves 4

Left: Mushroom Lasagne Rolls
Right: Chickpea and Pasta Patties

CHICKPEA AND PASTA PATTIES

75 g/2¹/₂ oz tiny pasta shapes
440 g/14 oz canned chickpeas,
drained and rinsed
¹/₂ cup/60 g/2 oz flour
1 onion, chopped
6 tablespoons chopped fresh parsley
1 clove garlic, crushed
1 teaspoon ground cumin
¹/₄ teaspoon dried chilli flakes
2 tablespoons lemon juice
1 egg, lightly beaten
seasoned flour
vegetable oil for shallow frying

1 Cook pasta in boiling water in a large saucepan following packet directions. Drain, rinse under cold running water and drain again.

2 Place chickpeas in a bowl and mash. Add pasta, flour, onion, parsley, garlic, cumin, chilli flakes, lemon juice and egg and mix to combine. Cover and chill for 1 hour.

3 Divide mixture into 14 portions and shape each into a patty. Roll each patty in seasoned flour to coat.

4 Heat 1 cm/¹/₂ in oil in a frying pan over a medium heat and cook patties, in batches, for 3 minutes each side or until golden and heated through. Drain on absorbent kitchen paper.

Makes 14 patties

For this recipe, use any one of a range of pastina, or 'tiny pasta', recommended for soups, such as risoni or orzo (rice shapes), ditalini (short tubes), anellini (tiny rings) or conchigliette (tiny shells). For a complete meal serve patties with a cucumber and yogurt salad and Lebanese or pitta bread.

HOT & SPICY

LASAGNE WITH NACHOS SAUCE

Oven temperature
180°C, 350°F, Gas 4

250 g/8 oz fresh lasagne sheets
vegetable oil for deep-frying
185 g/6 oz grated tasty cheese
(mature Cheddar)
1 avocado, sliced

NACHOS SAUCE
30 g/1 oz butter
1 onion, chopped
1 teaspoon Mexican chilli powder
440 g/14 oz canned red kidney beans,
drained and rinsed, lightly mashed
1 3/4 cups/440 g/14 oz sour cream

1 Cut lasagne into small triangles. Heat oil in a large saucepan until a cube of bread dropped in browns in 50 seconds. Add lasagne triangles and cook, in batches, for 2-3 minutes or until puffed and golden. Drain on absorbent kitchen paper and set aside.

2 To make sauce, melt butter in a saucepan over a medium heat, add onion and chilli powder and cook, stirring, for 5 minutes or until onion softens slightly. Remove from heat.

This dish makes a delicious and easy meal ideal for a family supper or casual entertaining.

3 Stir in red kidney beans and 1 1/4 cups/315 g/10 oz of the sour cream. Arrange lasagne triangles in a lightly greased ovenproof dish, spoon over sauce, sprinkle with cheese and bake for 15-20 minutes or until cheese melts and is golden. Serve topped with avocado and remaining sour cream.

Serves 6

MEXICANA PIZZA

Oven temperature
200°C, 400°F, Gas 6

200 g/6 1/2 oz elbow (short-cut)
macaroni
60 g/2 oz grated fresh Parmesan cheese
4 eggs, lightly beaten

PIZZA TOPPING
1/2 cup/125 mL/4 fl oz bottled tomato
pasta sauce
1/2 teaspoon Mexican chilli powder
2 red onions, sliced
125 g/4 oz button mushrooms, sliced
60 g/2 oz black olives, pitted
and quartered
250 g/8 oz grated mozzarella cheese

1 Cook pasta in boiling water in a large saucepan following packet directions. Drain, rinse under cold running water and drain again. Place pasta into a bowl, add Parmesan cheese and eggs and mix to combine. Press pasta mixture onto a lightly greased pizza tray and bake for 12-15 minutes or until firm to touch.

2 For topping, spread pasta base with pasta sauce, sprinkle with chilli powder, top with onions, mushrooms and olives and sprinkle with mozzarella cheese. Bake for 15-20 minutes longer or until cheese is golden and melted and vegetables are cooked.

Mexican chilli powder is primarily a blend of ground chillies, cumin and oregano.

Serves 6

Pasta-topped Spinach Casserole

PASTA-TOPPED SPINACH CASSEROLE

125 g/4 oz small pasta shells
30 g/1 oz butter
1 onion, chopped
1 clove garlic, crushed
2 bunches/1 kg/2 lb English spinach,
leaves shredded
2 x 440 g/14 oz canned tomatoes,
undrained and mashed
$^1/_2$ teaspoon cayenne pepper
1 cup/125 g/4 oz dried breadcrumbs
60 g/2 oz grated Romano or
Parmesan cheese
60 g/2 oz butter, melted

1 Cook pasta in boiling water in a large saucepan following packet directions. Drain and rinse under cold running water. Drain again and set aside.

2 Melt butter in a saucepan over a medium heat, add onion and garlic and cook, stirring, for 5 minutes or until onion is soft.

3 Add spinach, tomatoes and cayenne pepper to pan, bring to simmering and simmer for 15 minutes or until spinach is cooked and sauce reduces slightly. Spoon mixture into an 8 cup/2 litre/ $3^1/_2$ pt ovenproof dish.

4 Place breadcrumbs, Romano or Parmesan cheese, butter and pasta in a bowl and mix to combine. Spoon pasta mixture over tomato mixture and bake for 20-30 minutes or until top is golden and a crunchy crust forms.

Serves 4

Oven temperature
180°C, 350°F, Gas 4

For something different omit the cayenne pepper and fold 1-2 tablespoons of ready-made pesto into the spinach mixture.

GRILLED VEGETABLE SALAD

250 g/8 oz fresh angel's hair pasta
1 large eggplant (aubergine)
salt
1 large red pepper, seeded and quartered
1 large green pepper, seeded and quartered
4 spring onions, sliced diagonally

SESAME AND CHILLI DRESSING
2 fresh red chillies, seeded and diced
1 clove garlic, crushed
$^1/_2$ cup/125 mL/4 fl oz olive oil
$^1/_3$ cup/90 mL/3 fl oz soy sauce
2 tablespoons sesame oil
2 tablespoons honey
2 tablespoons red wine vinegar

1 Cook pasta in boiling water in a large saucepan following packet directions. Drain and rinse under cold running water. Drain again and set aside.

2 Cut eggplant (aubergine) into 1 cm/$^1/_2$ in thick slices and place in a colander. Sprinkle with salt and set aside for 1 hour. Rinse eggplant (aubergine) under cold running water, then pat dry with absorbent kitchen paper.

3 To make dressing, place chillies, garlic, olive oil, soy sauce, sesame oil, honey and vinegar in a bowl and whisk to combine.

4 Brush eggplant (aubergine) slices with some of the dressing and cook under a preheated hot grill for 5 minutes each side or until golden. Set aside to cool, then cut into strips.

5 Place red and green pepper quarters, skin side up, under a hot grill and cook for 5-10 minutes or until skins are blistered and charred. Place peppers in a plastic food or paper bag and set aside until cool enough to handle. Remove skins and cut flesh into chunks.

6 Place pasta, eggplant (aubergine), red and green peppers and spring onions in a large bowl and toss gently. Pour over remaining dressing and toss to coat pasta and vegetables. Cover and chill until required.

Serves 6

This pretty pasta dish is delightful for casual entertaining. Serve with hot bread flavoured with cheese and herbs.

Grilled Vegetable Salad

INDIAN VEGETABLE PASTIES

Oven temperature
200°C, 400°F, Gas 6

Serve these hot and spicy
pasties warm with a cooling
accompaniment of yogurt
and cucumber sauce.

750 g/1¹/₂ lb prepared puff pastry
1 egg, lightly beaten

SPICY VEGETABLE FILLING
60 g/2 oz small elbow (short-cut)
macaroni or other small pasta shapes
1 tablespoon vegetable oil
1 small onion, chopped
1 clove garlic, crushed
2 teaspoons finely grated fresh ginger
2 teaspoons cumin seeds
2 teaspoons coriander seeds
1 tablespoon garam masala
2 teaspoons ground turmeric
¹/₂ teaspoon chilli powder
60 g/2 oz shelled fresh or frozen peas
1 large tomato, peeled and diced

1   To make filling, cook pasta in
boiling water in a large saucepan
following packet directions. Drain and
rinse under cold running water. Drain
again and set aside.

2   Heat oil in a frying pan over a low
heat, add onion, garlic, ginger, cumin,
coriander, garam masala, turmeric and
chilli powder and cook, stirring, for
5 minutes or until onion softens slightly.

3   Stir in peas and tomato, bring to
simmering and simmer for 10 minutes
or until any liquid evaporates and
mixture thickens. Stir in pasta and set
aside to cool.

4   Roll out pastry to 5 mm/¹/₄ in thick
and using a 7.5 cm/3 in round cutter,
cut out 40 rounds. Place a teaspoon of
filling on each pastry round, fold pastry
over filling to form a half-moon shape
and pinch edges together to seal. Brush
each pastry with egg and place on
lightly greased baking trays. Bake for
12-15 minutes or until pasties are
puffed and golden.

Makes 40 pasties

Indian Vegetable Pasties

Spicy Tomato Pilau

SPICY TOMATO PILAU

1 tablespoon vegetable oil
90 g/3 oz raw cashews
2 onions, sliced
3 teaspoons hot Madras curry powder
2 teaspoons ground turmeric
2 carrots, diced
125 g/4 oz risoni or orzo pasta (small rice shapes)
440 g/14 oz canned tomatoes, undrained and mashed
1¹/₂ cups/375 mL/12 fl oz vegetable stock
125 g/4 oz frozen peas or frozen mixed vegetables

1   Heat oil in a saucepan over a medium heat, add cashews and cook, stirring, for 2 minutes or until golden. Remove cashews and drain on absorbent kitchen paper. Add onions to pan and cook, stirring, for 5 minutes or until onions soften slightly. Add curry powder and turmeric and cook, stirring, for 1 minute.

2   Add carrots, pasta, tomatoes and stock to pan and bring to simmering. Cover and simmer over a low heat for 15 minutes. Stir in peas or vegetables, cover and cook for 5 minutes longer. Remove cover and cook for 5 minutes or until most of the liquid evaporates. Stir in cashews and serve immediately.

Serves 6

A handful of sultanas, chopped raisins or dried apricots makes a tasty addition to this dish.

CARROT, LENTIL AND PASTA SOUP

125 g/4 oz cresti di gallo pasta
250 g/8 oz yellow lentils
1 tablespoon olive oil
2 carrots, roughly chopped
2 onions, chopped
2 cloves garlic, crushed
1 tablespoon garam masala
10 cups/2.5 litres/4^1/$_4$ pt vegetable
stock
2 tablespoons chopped fresh coriander

Cresti di gallo or 'cock's crests' are so named because it resembles a cock's comb. About 3 cm/ 1^1/$_4$ in long, it is slightly curved with a curly outer rib along the back. Any small pasta shape suitable for soups, such as elbow (short-cut) macaroni can be substituted.

1 Cook pasta in a large saucepan of boiling water following packet directions. Drain and rinse under cold running water. Drain again and set aside. Wash lentils, drain and set aside.

2 Heat oil in a saucepan over a medium heat, add carrots, onions and garlic and cook, stirring occasionally, for 10 minutes or until vegetables are soft. Add garam masala and cook, stirring, for 1 minute longer.

3 Add lentils and stock to pan and bring to the boil. Reduce heat and simmer, stirring occasionally, for 30-40 minutes or until lentils are cooked. Cool slightly.

4 Purée soup mixture, in batches, in a food processor or blender. Return purée to a clean saucepan, stir in pasta and cook over a low heat, stirring, for 5 minutes or until soup is hot. Stir in coriander and serve immediately.

Serves 6

CURRIED CHEESE DAMPER

Oven temperature
200°C, 400°F, Gas 6

90 g/3 oz tiny pasta shapes of your choice
4 cups/500 g/1 lb self-raising flour
1 teaspoon salt
30 g/1 oz butter
1 cup/250 mL/8 fl oz milk
^{1}/$_2$ cup/125 mL/4 fl oz water

CURRIED CHEESE TOPPING
125 g/4 oz grated vintage mature
Cheddar cheese
45 g/1^1/$_2$ oz butter, softened
3 teaspoons hot curry powder
1 teaspoon black mustard seeds

When choosing pasta for this recipe, refer to the tip on page 9. Cooked pasta adds moisture and an interesting texture to this quick bread. Delicious served warm with soups and casseroles.

1 Cook pasta in boiling water in a large saucepan following packet directions. Drain and rinse under cold running water. Drain again and set aside.

2 Sift flour and salt together into a bowl, then rub in butter until mixture resembles coarse breadcrumbs. Make a well in centre of flour mixture, pour in milk and water, add pasta and using a knife mix quickly to form a soft dough. Knead briefly. Shape dough into a 20 cm/8 in round and place on a lightly greased baking tray.

3 To make topping, place cheese, butter and curry powder in a bowl and mix to combine. Sprinkle damper with topping and mustard seeds. Using a floured knife cut a cross in the top.

4 Bake for 25 minutes, then reduce oven temperature to 180°C /350°F/ Gas 4 and bake for 10-15 minutes longer or until damper sounds hollow when tapped on the base. Stand on tray for 10 minutes. Serve warm or cold.

Makes 1 damper

Curried Cheese Damper,
Carrot, Lentil and Pasta Soup

Above: Wholemeal Pasta Curry
Right: Penne with Spicy Tomato Sauce

WHOLEMEAL PASTA CURRY

1 tablespoon vegetable oil
2 onions, chopped
1 clove garlic, crushed
¹/2 teaspoon finely grated fresh ginger
1 teaspoon ground turmeric
1 teaspoon ground cumin
¹/2 teaspoon chilli powder
¹/2 cauliflower, broken into
small florets
155 g/5 oz green beans, trimmed
125 g/4 oz wholemeal pasta
of your choice
4 cups/1 litre/1³/4 pt vegetable stock

1   Heat oil in a saucepan over a medium heat, add onions, garlic and ginger and cook, stirring, for 5 minutes or until onion softens slightly. Add turmeric, cumin and chilli powder and cook, stirring, for 2 minutes.

2   Stir in cauliflower, beans, pasta and stock, bring to simmering and simmer for 15-20 minutes or until vegetables and pasta are tender.

Serves 4

PENNE WITH SPICY TOMATO SAUCE

375 g/12 oz penne

SPICY TOMATO SAUCE
1 tablespoon olive oil
2 onions, chopped
1 clove garlic, crushed
1 teaspoon ground cumin
$^1/_2$ teaspoon chilli powder
1 kg/2 lb ripe tomatoes, peeled
and chopped
freshly ground black pepper
2 tablespoons chopped fresh parsley

1   Cook pasta in boiling water in a large saucepan following packet directions. Drain, set aside and keep warm.

2   To make sauce, heat oil in a frying pan over a medium heat, add onions and garlic and cook, stirring, for 5 minutes or until onions soften slightly.

3   Add cumin and chilli powder to pan and cook, stirring, for 2 minutes. Add tomatoes and black pepper to taste, bring to simmering and simmer for 6-8 minutes or until sauce thickens and tomatoes are cooked. Stir in parsley. Spoon sauce over pasta and toss to combine.

Serves 4

Use plum (egg or Italian) tomatoes when in season for the best flavour and a smoother consistency.

Coconut Vegetable Curry

1 tablespoon vegetable oil
1 onion, sliced
1 clove garlic, crushed
1 tablespoon hot Madras curry powder
$^1/_4$ teaspoon chilli powder
$1^1/_2$ cups/375 mL/12 fl oz coconut
cream
3 cups/750 mL/$1^1/_4$ pt water
2 potatoes, cubed
250 g/8 oz sweet potato, cubed
125 g/4 oz shelled fresh or frozen peas
125 g/4 oz risoni or orzo pasta (small
rice shapes)
2 teaspoons lemon juice
1 tablespoon chopped fresh coriander

1   Heat oil in a large saucepan over a medium heat, add onion and garlic and cook, stirring, for 5 minutes or until onion softens slightly. Add curry and chilli powders and cook, stirring, for 1 minute longer.

2   Stir coconut cream, water, potatoes, sweet potato, peas, pasta and lemon juice into pan and bring to the boil. Reduce heat and simmer, stirring occasionally, for 20 minutes or until vegetables and pasta are cooked. Stir in coriander and serve.

Serves 4

For a more substantial meal try serving this curry with wedges of grilled polenta or steamed fragrant rice.

Pasta with Hot Curry Sauce

375 g/12 oz large fusilli pasta
(spirals or twists)

HOT CURRY SAUCE
1 tablespoon vegetable oil
1 onion, thinly sliced
1 clove garlic, crushed
1 teaspoon finely grated fresh ginger
2 teaspoons hot curry paste
1 teaspoon ground turmeric
$1^1/_4$ cups/315 mL/10 fl oz cream
(double)
125 g/4 oz frozen mixed vegetables
(carrots, peas, sweet corn kernels)
$^1/_2$ cup/125 mL/4 fl oz water
1 teaspoon finely grated lemon rind

1   Cook pasta in boiling water in a large saucepan following packet directions. Drain, set aside and keep warm.

2   To make sauce, heat oil in a frying pan over a medium heat, add onion, garlic and ginger and cook, stirring occasionally, for 8 minutes or until onion softens. Add curry paste and turmeric and cook over a low heat, stirring, for 2 minutes.

3   Stir cream, vegetables, water and lemon rind into pan, bring to simmering and simmer for 5 minutes or until vegetables are cooked. Spoon sauce over pasta and toss to combine.

Serves 4

A sprinkling of chopped fresh coriander or mint makes a tasty addition to this dish.

Coconut Vegetable Curry, Pasta with Hot Curry Sauce

ORIENTAL
INFLUENCE

Vegetable Laksa

1 tablespoon vegetable oil
2 onions, finely chopped
2 cloves garlic, crushed
1 teaspoon finely grated fresh ginger
2 teaspoons ground turmeric
1$\frac{1}{2}$ teaspoons chilli paste
(sambal oelek)
6 cups/1.5 litres/2$\frac{1}{2}$ pt vegetable
stock
155 mL/5 fl oz coconut milk
155 g/5 oz dried flat egg noodles
125 g/4 oz bean sprouts
4 spring onions, sliced

1   Heat oil in a saucepan over a medium heat, add onions, garlic and ginger and cook, stirring occasionally, for 10 minutes or until onions are soft. Add turmeric and cook, stirring, for 1 minute longer.

2   Stir in chilli paste (sambal oelek), stock and coconut milk and bring to the boil. Reduce heat and simmer for 5 minutes. Add noodles, bring back to the boil and boil for 5 minutes or until noodles are cooked. Stir in bean sprouts and spring onions and cook for 1 minute longer.

Serves 6

To serve, ladle soup into bowls and top with chopped fresh chilli if liked.

Thai-style Noodle Soup

5 cups/1.2 litres/2 pt vegetable stock
125 g/4 oz oyster mushrooms, halved
6 spring onions, cut into
2.5 cm/1 in lengths
2 teaspoons finely grated fresh ginger
$\frac{1}{4}$ teaspoon chilli paste (sambal oelek)
2 tablespoons soy sauce
155 g/5 oz fresh thin egg noodles
90 g/3 oz bean sprouts
2 tablespoons chopped fresh coriander

1   Heat stock in a saucepan over a medium heat, add mushrooms, spring onions, ginger, chilli paste (sambal oelek) and soy sauce and bring to the boil. Reduce heat and simmer for 5 minutes.

2   Add noodles, return to the boil and simmer for 2-3 minutes or until noodles are cooked. Stir in bean sprouts and coriander. Serve immediately.

Serves 6

Oriental egg noodles vary in thickness from fine strands to pieces as thick as a shoelace, with a texture and taste similar to Italian spaghetti, being made with the same ingredients. Purchase fresh or dried noodles from Oriental food stores and supermarkets. Fresh noodles are best cooked as soon as possible but can be kept refrigerated for up to 4 days.

VEGETABLE AND PEANUT WONTONS

60 g/2 oz cellophane noodles
125 g/4 oz bean sprouts
45 g/1¹/₂ oz unsalted peanuts,
chopped
1 carrot, grated
2 spring onions, sliced
1 teaspoon finely grated fresh ginger
2 teaspoons soy sauce
50 wonton wrappers each
12.5 cm/5 in square
2 teaspoons cornflour blended with
2 tablespoons water
vegetable oil for deep-frying

1   Cover noodles with hot water and soak for 2-3 minutes or until soft. Drain well and chop roughly.

2   Place noodles, bean sprouts, peanuts, carrot, spring onions, ginger, and soy sauce in a bowl and mix to combine.

3   Place a heaped teaspoon of vegetable mixture in the centre of each wonton wrapper. Brush edges with cornflour mixture and gather up edges to make a bundle. Twist top lightly.

4   Heat oil in a large saucepan over a high heat until a cube of bread dropped in browns in 50 seconds. Cook wontons, a few at a time, for 3-4 minutes or until golden. Drain on absorbent kitchen paper and serve immediately.

Makes approximately 50

Cellophane noodles are transparent noodles made from mung beans. Serve wontons with sweet chilli sauce for dipping.

HOT CHILLI AND BASIL PASTA

315 g/10 dried tagliatelle
3 tablespoons vegetable oil
315 g/10 oz broccoli florets
1 red pepper, sliced
2 cloves garlic, crushed
2 fresh red chillies, seeded
and chopped
3 tablespoons chopped fresh basil
$^1/4$ cup/60 mL/2 fl oz soy sauce
$^1/4$ cup/60 mL/2 fl oz Chinese rice wine

1 Cook pasta in boiling water in a large saucepan following packet directions. Drain, set aside and keep warm.

2 Heat 1 tablespoon oil in a wok or frying pan over a medium heat, add broccoli, red pepper, garlic and chillies and stir-fry for 2 minutes. Stir in basil, soy sauce, rice wine and remaining oil, bring to the boil, then reduce heat and simmer for 1 minute. Add pasta and toss to combine. Serve immediately.

Serves 4

Serve in shallow pasta plates so that none of the liquid is lost.

NOODLES WITH PLUM SAUCE

185 g/6 oz dried egg noodles
1 tablespoon vegetable oil
250 g/8 oz snow peas (mangetout)
2 carrots, sliced diagonally
1 onion, sliced
1 green pepper, chopped
1 clove garlic, crushed
$^3/4$ teaspoon five spice powder
$^1/2$ cup/125 mL/4 fl oz Chinese
plum sauce
2 tablespoons soy sauce

1 Cook noodles in boiling water in a large saucepan following packet directions. Drain, set aside and keep warm.

2 Heat oil in a wok or frying pan over a medium heat, add snow peas (mangetout), carrots, onion, green pepper and garlic and stir-fry for 2-3 minutes or until vegetables are just cooked. Stir in five spice powder, plum sauce and soy sauce, bring to simmering and simmer for 1 minute. Add pasta, toss to combine and serve immediately.

Serves 4

This recipe is also good made with any of the following – fettuccine, tagliatelle, linguini, papardelle, spaghetti or quick-cooking Oriental noodles.

Noodles with Plum Sauce, Hot Chilli and Basil Pasta

Oven temperature
180°C, 350°F, Gas 4

2 large eggplant (aubergines)
salt
60 g/2 oz elbow (short-cut) macaroni
or other small pasta shapes
30 g/1 oz butter
60 g/2 oz pine nuts
125 g/4 oz button mushrooms,
chopped
1 red pepper, chopped
1 teaspoon finely grated fresh ginger
1 tablespoon hoisin sauce
1 tablespoon soy sauce
vegetable oil for shallow frying

Delicious served with a
salad of mixed greens and
cherry tomatoes.

1   Cut eggplant (aubergines) lengthwise
into 5 mm/¹/4 in thick slices. Place in
a colander, sprinkle with salt and
drain for 30 minutes. Rinse eggplant
(aubergines) under cold running water
and pat dry with absorbent kitchen
paper. Set aside.

2   Cook pasta in boiling water in a large
saucepan following packet directions.
Drain and rinse under cold running
water. Drain again and set aside.

3   Melt butter in a frying pan over a
medium heat, add pine nuts and cook,
stirring, for 2-3 minutes or until golden.
Remove nuts from pan and drain on
absorbent kitchen paper. Add
mushrooms, red pepper and ginger to
pan and cook, stirring, for 2 minutes.
Return pine nuts to pan, then add
pasta, hoisin sauce and soy sauce and
bring to simmering. Remove pan from
heat and set aside.

4   Heat 2.5 cm/1 in oil in a frying pan
over a medium heat and cook eggplant
(aubergine) slices, in batches, for
2-3 minutes each side or until golden.
Drain eggplant (aubergine) on
absorbent kitchen paper and set aside.

5   Divide mushroom mixture evenly
between eggplant (aubergine) slices, roll
up and secure with wooden toothpicks
or cocktail sticks. Place rolls on a lightly
greased baking tray and bake for
10 minutes or until heated through.

Serves 6

Left: Oriental Rolls
Right: Black Bean and Bok Choy Stir-fry

Black Bean and Bok Choy Stir-fry

2 tablespoons salted black beans
250 g/8 oz dried flat egg noodles
2 tablespoons vegetable oil
250 g/ 8 oz bok choy, leaves
separated and trimmed
155 g/5 oz snow peas (mangetout)
1 onion, cut into wedges and
layers separated
1 clove garlic, crushed
1 teaspoon finely grated fresh ginger
1 fresh red chilli, seeded and diced
$^1/_3$ cup/90 mL/3 fl oz dry sherry
$^1/_4$ cup/60 mL/2 fl oz soy sauce

1 Place black beans in a small bowl, cover with cold water and soak for 10 minutes. Drain beans, mash lightly and set aside.

2 Cook noodles in boiling water in a large saucepan following packet directions. Drain, set aside and keep warm.

3 Heat 1 tablespoon oil in a wok over a medium heat, add bok choy and cook, turning several times, for 2-3 minutes. Remove from pan and set aside. Heat remaining oil in wok, add snow peas (mangetout), onion, garlic, ginger and chilli and stir-fry for 1 minute or until snow peas (mangetout) change colour.

4 Add black beans, sherry and soy sauce to wok and bring to the boil. Reduce heat and simmer for 1 minute. Add noodles and bok choy and toss lightly to combine. Heat for 1-2 minutes and serve immediately.

Serves 4

Bok choy, also known as pak choy, is a member of the cabbage family with succulent white ribs and delicate green leaves. Chinese broccoli and English spinach are interchangeable with bok choy in this dish.
Any leftover black beans and liquid will keep indefinitely in a sealed container in the refrigerator.

PASTA AND VEGETABLE STIR-FRY

30 g/1 oz dried Chinese mushrooms
315 g/10 oz large fusilli pasta (spirals
or twists)
3 tablespoons vegetable oil
60 g/2 oz raw cashews
2 cloves garlic, crushed
1 teaspoon finely grated fresh ginger
315 g/10 oz Chinese cabbage, sliced
90 g/3 oz snow peas (mangetout)
6 spring onions, sliced diagonally
3 tablespoons Chinese rice wine
2 tablespoons light soy sauce
1 tablespoon sweet chilli sauce

Look for black fungi in Oriental food stores and at greengrocers. If unavailable, substitute with any fresh mushroom of your choice, or use a combination of mushrooms.

1   Place mushrooms in a bowl cover with boiling water and soak for 10 minutes or until mushrooms are tender. Drain, remove stems and cut mushrooms into thin strips.

2   Cook pasta in boiling water in a large saucepan, following packet directions. Drain, set aside and keep warm.

3   Heat 1 tablespoon oil in a wok over a medium heat, add cashews and stir-fry for 1-2 minutes or until golden. Remove from pan and drain on absorbent kitchen paper.

4   Heat remaining oil in pan, add garlic and ginger and stir-fry for 1 minute. Add cabbage, snow peas (mangetout), spring onions and mushrooms and stir-fry for 2-3 minutes or until vegetables change colour. Stir in rice wine, soy sauce and chilli sauce, bring to simmering and simmer for 1 minute. Add cashews and pasta and toss to combine.

Serves 4

FRIED NOODLES

185 g/6 oz dried thin egg noodles
2 tablespoons vegetable oil
4 eggs, lightly beaten
2 carrots, diced
2 zucchini (courgettes), diced
125 g/4 oz mushrooms, diced
8 spring onions, sliced
60 g/2 oz shelled fresh or frozen
peas, cooked
1 teaspoon finely grated fresh ginger
2 teaspoons sesame oil
2 tablespoons soy sauce

This is a delicious variation on traditional fried rice. It can also be served as an accompaniment in which case it would serve six.

1   Cook noodles in boiling water in a large saucepan following packet directions. Drain, set aside and keep warm.

2   Heat 1 tablespoon oil in a wok or frying pan over a medium heat, pour in beaten eggs and cook until underside is golden. Turn over and cook until other side is golden. Remove omelette from wok, chop roughly and set aside.

3   Heat remaining oil in pan over a medium heat, add carrots, zucchini (courgettes), mushrooms, spring onions, peas and ginger and stir-fry for 2-3 minutes or until vegetables are just cooked.

4   Add pasta, omelette, sesame oil and soy sauce and toss to combine. Cook for 1-2 minutes or until heated through and serve immediately.

Serves 4

Fried Noodles, Pasta and Vegetable Stir-fry

Pasta with Mixed Mushrooms

315 g/10 oz dried tagliatelle

MIXED MUSHROOM SAUCE
75 g/2$^{1}/_{2}$ oz dried Chinese mushrooms
30 g/1 oz butter
8 spring onions, cut into
2.5 cm/1 in pieces
1 clove garlic, crushed
155 g/5 oz oyster mushrooms, sliced
155 g/5 oz button mushrooms, sliced
1 cup/250 mL/8 fl oz water
$^{1}/_{2}$ cup/125 mL/4 fl oz coconut cream
2 tablespoons sesame oil

1   Cook pasta in boiling water in a large saucepan following packet directions. Drain, set aside and keep warm.

2   To make sauce, place Chinese mushrooms in a bowl, cover with boiling water and soak for 10 minutes or until tender. Drain, remove stems and cut mushrooms into thin strips.

3   Melt butter in a wok or frying pan over a medium heat, add spring onions and garlic and stir-fry for 1 minute. Add oyster, button and Chinese mushrooms and stir-fry for 3 minutes or until mushrooms are soft. Stir in water, coconut cream and sesame oil, bring to simmering and simmer for 1 minute. Spoon sauce over pasta and toss.

Serves 4

ORIENTAL-STYLE KEBABS

Left: Pasta with Mixed Mushrooms
Above: Oriental-style Kebabs

125 g/4 oz large pasta shapes of your choice
155 g/5 oz tofu, cut into
1 cm/¹/₂ in cubes
185 g/6 oz broccoli florets, blanched
125 g/4 oz fresh baby sweet corn,
blanched or canned baby sweet corn,
cut into 5 cm/2 in lengths
4 spring onions, cut into
2.5 cm/1 in pieces

HOISIN MARINADE
1 clove garlic, crushed
1 teaspoon finely grated fresh ginger
¹/₃ cup/90 mL/3 fl oz hoisin sauce
2 tablespoons sesame oil
2 tablespoons soy sauce
1 tablespoon vegetable oil

1 Cook pasta in boiling water in a large saucepan following packet directions. Drain, rinse under cold running water and drain again.

2 Place pasta, tofu, broccoli, sweet corn and spring onions in a large bowl. Set aside.

3 To make marinade, place garlic, ginger, hoisin sauce, sesame oil, soy sauce and vegetable oil in a bowl and whisk to combine. Spoon marinade over pasta mixture and toss. Cover and marinate in the refrigerator for 1 hour.

4 Drain pasta mixture and reserve marinade. Thread pasta, vegetables and tofu, alternately, onto six oiled skewers. Brush with reserved marinade and cook under a preheated medium grill, brushing frequently with marinade, for 10-15 minutes or until vegetables are cooked.

Serves 6

Shell or wheel-shaped pasta is best for these kebabs as they are easy to thread onto the skewers and won't fall off.

VEGETABLES IN GREEN CURRY SAUCE

315 g/10 oz dried pasta of your choice

GREEN CURRY SAUCE
1 teaspoon brown sugar
1 tablespoon green curry paste
1¹/₂ cups/375 mL/12 fl oz coconut milk
2 tablespoons lemon juice
2 zucchini (courgettes), sliced
185 g/6 oz green beans, halved
1 green pepper, chopped
125 g/4 oz bean sprouts
3 tablespoons shredded fresh basil

1 Cook pasta in boiling water in a large saucepan following packet directions. Drain, set aside and keep warm.

2 To make sauce, place sugar, curry paste, coconut milk and lemon juice in a saucepan and bring to the boil over a medium heat. Add zucchini (courgettes), beans and green pepper, bring to simmering and simmer for 5 minutes or until vegetables are just cooked.

3 Stir in bean sprouts and basil and cook for 1 minute longer. Spoon sauce over pasta and toss to combine.

Serves 4

FETTUCCINE WITH COCONUT SAUCE

375 g/12 oz fresh mixed fettuccine

COCONUT CORIANDER SAUCE
1 cup/250 mL/8 fl oz coconut milk or coconut cream
3 tablespoons chopped fresh coriander
2 tablespoons sweet chilli sauce
1 clove garlic, crushed

1 Cook pasta in boiling water in a large saucepan following packet directions. Drain, set aside and keep warm.

2 To make sauce, place coconut milk or cream, coriander, chilli sauce and garlic in a saucepan, bring to simmering over a medium heat and simmer for 2 minutes. Add pasta to sauce and toss to coat with sauce.

Serves 4

Any type of pasta can be used for this dish, however, it looks very attractive when made with a combination of red, green and white fettuccine.

*Vegetables in Green Curry Sauce,
Fettuccine with Coconut Sauce*

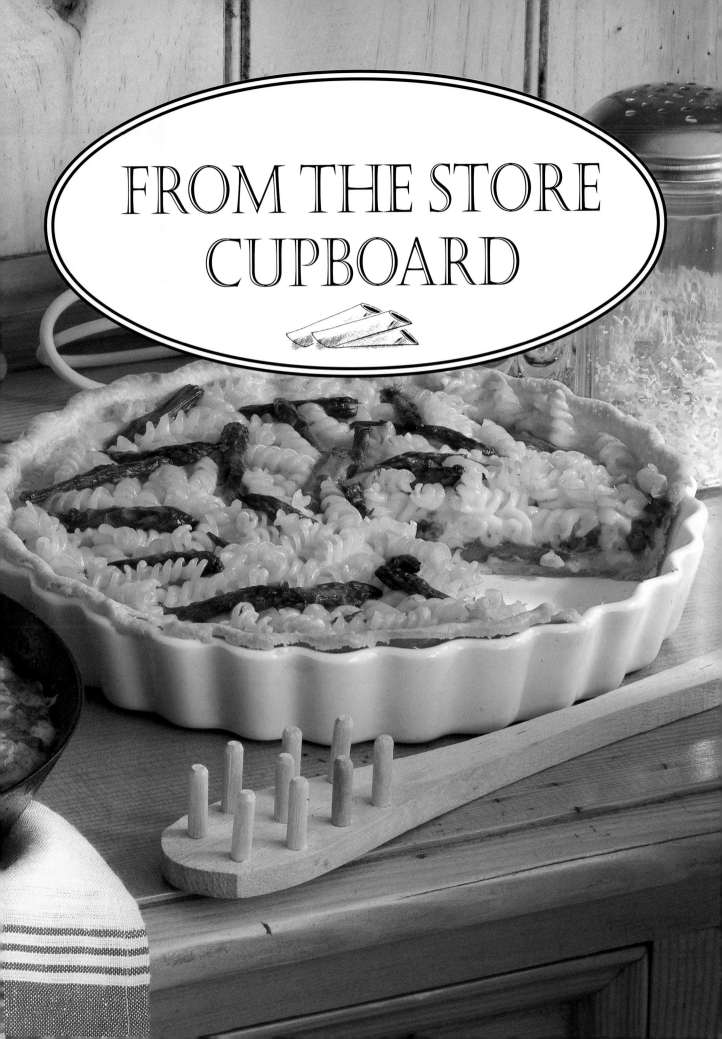

FROM THE STORE CUPBOARD

PASTA AND SUN-DRIED TOMATO CAKE

315 g/10 oz spaghetti
185 g/6 oz marinated or canned
artichoke hearts, drained and chopped
90 g/3 oz sun-dried tomatoes in oil,
drained and chopped
3 spring onions, chopped
2 tablespoons chopped fresh basil or
2 teaspoons dried basil
6 eggs, lightly beaten
250 g/8 oz grated tasty cheese
(mature Cheddar)
freshly ground black pepper

Convenient items from the delicatessen team with inexpensive eggs and cheese to turn pasta into a special meal.
Marinated artichoke hearts are available from some Italian food shops or you can marinate canned artichoke hearts in a mixture of olive oil, lemon juice and mixed herbs.

1 Cook pasta in boiling water in a large saucepan following packet directions. Drain, rinse under cold running water and drain again.

2 Place pasta, artichoke hearts, sun-dried tomatoes, spring onions, basil, eggs, half the cheese and black pepper to taste in a bowl and mix to combine.

3 Pour mixture into a greased 25 cm/10 in frying pan and cook over a medium-low heat for 8-10 minutes or until firm. Sprinkle with remaining cheese and cook under a preheated hot grill for 3-5 minutes or until cheese melts and top is golden.

Serves 6

ASPARAGUS AND PASTA QUICHE

Oven temperature
180°C, 350°F, Gas 4

90 g/3 oz small pasta shapes,
such as elbow (short-cut) macaroni,
shells or twists
155 g/5 oz prepared shortcrust pastry
125 g/4 oz Gruyère cheese,
thinly sliced
350 g/11 oz canned asparagus tips,
well-drained
3 eggs
1 1/4 cups/315 mL/10 fl oz cream
(double)
pinch grated nutmeg
freshly ground black pepper

A mixture of cream and milk could be used instead of all cream. It is important to partially bake the pastry case to prevent the pastry from becoming soggy.

1 Cook pasta in boiling water in a large saucepan following packet directions. Drain and rinse under cold running water. Drain again and set aside.

2 Roll out pastry to 5 mm/1/4 in thick and use to line a 23 cm/9 in flan tin. Prick base and sides of pastry case with fork, line with nonstick baking paper and fill with uncooked rice. Bake for 15 minutes or until pastry is lightly browned. Remove paper and rice and set aside to cool.

3 Arrange cheese over base of pastry case then top with asparagus and pasta.

4 Place eggs, cream, nutmeg and black pepper to taste in a bowl and whisk to combine. Carefully pour egg mixture into pastry case, then bake for 30-40 minutes or until filling is firm. Serve hot, warm or cold.

Serves 6

Pasta and Corn Chowder

30 g/1 oz butter
1 onion, chopped
2 potatoes, peeled and chopped
125 g/4 oz sprial pasta
1 bay leaf
4 cups/1 litre/1³/4 pt vegetable stock
freshly ground black pepper
2 tablespoons flour
2 cups/500 mL/16 fl oz milk
315 g/10 oz canned sweet corn
kernels, drained
¹/4 teaspoon dried thyme leaves

1   Melt butter in a saucepan over a medium heat, add onion and cook, stirring occasionally, for 5 minutes or until onion is soft. Add potatoes, pasta, bay leaf and stock and bring to the boil. Reduce heat and simmer for 15 minutes or until potatoes and pasta are cooked. Season to taste with black pepper.

2   Mix flour with a little milk to make a smooth paste. Remove pan from heat, gradually stir in flour mixture, return pan to heat and cook, stirring, until soup returns to simmering.

3   Stir in sweet corn, thyme and remaining milk, return to simmering and simmer for 3 minutes longer.

Serves 6

Any variety of small pasta shapes could be used for this easy soup. For a complete meal serve with crusty bread and a tossed green salad.

MINTED PEA AND CORN BAKE

Oven temperature
180°C, 350°F, Gas 4

185 g/6 oz elbow (short-cut) macaroni
30 g/1 oz packet French onion soup mix
2 tablespoons flour blended with
$^{1}/_{4}$ cup/60 mL/2 fl oz water
315 g/10 oz canned creamed sweet corn
315 g/10 oz canned red kidney beans,
drained and rinsed
250 g/8 oz frozen minted peas
1 teaspoon lemon (citrus) pepper
200 g/6$^{1}/_{2}$ oz packet corn chips
125 g/4 oz grated tasty cheese
(mature Cheddar)
$^{1}/_{2}$ teaspoon ground paprika

1 Cook pasta in boiling water in a large saucepan following packet directions. Drain, set aside and keep warm.

2 Make soup according to packet directions – but use only 1 cup/250 mL/ 8 fl oz water. Stir flour mixture into soup mixture and cook over a medium heat, stirring constantly, until soup comes to the boil. Reduce heat and simmer for 2 minutes.

3 Stir pasta, sweet corn, red kidney beans, peas and lemon (citrus) pepper into soup. Spoon mixture into a greased ovenproof dish. Top with corn chips and sprinkle with cheese and paprika. Bake for 30-40 minutes or until top is golden.

Serves 8

QUICK TOMATO AND BEAN LASAGNE

Oven temperature
190°C, 375°F, Gas 5

750 g/1$^{1}/_{2}$ lb bottled tomato
pasta sauce
750 g/1$^{1}/_{2}$ lb canned three bean mix,
drained and rinsed
12 sheets instant (no precooking
required) lasagne
90 g/3 oz grated tasty cheese
(mature Cheddar)

WHITE SAUCE
45 g/1$^{1}/_{2}$ oz butter
$^{1}/_{4}$ cup/30 g/1 oz flour
2 cups/500 mL/16 fl oz milk
90 g/3 oz grated tasty cheese
(mature Cheddar)
pinch ground nutmeg
freshly ground pepper

1 Place pasta sauce and beans in a bowl and mix to combine.

2 To make sauce, melt butter in a saucepan over a low heat, stir in flour and cook, stirring for 1 minute. Remove pan from heat and gradually stir in milk. Return pan to heat and cook over a medium heat, stirring, until sauce boils and thickens. Stir in cheese and nutmeg and black pepper to taste.

3 To assemble, line base of a greased 18 x 30 cm/7 x 12 in ovenproof dish with one-third of the lasagne. Spoon over half the bean mixture then half the sauce. Repeat layers, finishing with a layer of lasagne and sauce. Sprinkle with cheese and bake for 40-45 minutes.

Serves 6

Stand lasagne in a warm place for 20-30 minutes before cutting to allow layers to settle.
For more information about three bean mix see tip on page 38.

Pancakes with Pesto and Olives

6 tablespoons ready-made pesto
1 red pepper, chopped
60 g/2 oz black or green olives, pitted
and quartered
155 g/5 oz feta cheese, crumbled

WHOLEMEAL PANCAKES
125 g/4 oz tiny pasta shapes
$^2/_3$ cup/170 mL/$5^1/_2$ fl oz milk
1 teaspoon vinegar
1 egg, lightly beaten
1 cup/155 g/5 oz wholemeal flour
$^1/_4$ teaspoon bicarbonate of soda
pinch sugar
pinch salt
15 g/$^1/_2$ oz butter

When choosing pasta for this recipe refer to the tip on page 9. Feta cheese does not melt completely. For a variation, use bottled tomato pasta sauce in place of pesto and green pepper instead of red pepper.

1 To make pancakes, cook pasta in boiling water in a large saucepan following packet directions. Drain and rinse under cold running water. Drain again and set aside.

2 Place milk, vinegar and egg in a jug and mix to combine. Sift flour, bicarbonate of soda, sugar and salt together into a bowl. Make a well in centre of flour mixture, pour in milk mixture and mix until smooth. Stir in pasta.

3 Melt butter in a frying pan over a low heat, pour one-sixth of the pancake mixture into pan and cook for 2-3 minutes or until bubbles appear on surface of pancake and base is golden. Turn and cook for 2-3 minutes longer. Remove pancake from pan, set aside and keep warm. Repeat with remaining pancake mixture to make 6 pancakes.

4 Spread each pancake with 1 tablespoon pesto, then top with red pepper and olives and scatter with feta cheese. Place pancakes under a preheated hot grill and cook for 3-4 minutes or until cheese softens and starts to brown.

Serves 6

Left: Pancakes with Pesto and Olives
Right: Beetroot and Walnut Salad

BEETROOT AND WALNUT SALAD

250 g/8 oz large pasta shells
2 oranges, peeled and segmented
75 g/2^1/$_2$ oz walnut pieces
440 g/14 oz canned or bottled whole
baby beetroot, drained and quartered

BALSAMIC AND ORANGE
DRESSING
1 tablespoon chopped fresh parsley
^{1}/$_4$ cup/60 mL/2 fl oz olive oil
1 tablespoon balsamic vinegar
1 tablespoon orange juice
1 teaspoon French mustard
freshly ground black pepper

1   Cook pasta in boiling water in a large
saucepan following packet directions.
Drain, rinse under cold running water
and drain again. Place in a salad bowl.

2   Add oranges and walnuts to pasta
and toss gently to combine.

3   To make dressing, place parsley,
oil, vinegar, orange juice, mustard and
black pepper to taste in a bowl and
whisk to combine. Spoon dressing over
pasta and toss. Just prior to serving, top
with beetroot.

Serves 6

Wine vinegar can be
substituted for balsamic.
Add beetroot just before
serving to prevent it from
discolouring the pasta.

CRESTS WITH MUSHROOMS

375 g/12 oz cresti di gallo pasta

MUSHROOM AND
PAPRIKA SAUCE
30 g/1 oz butter
125 g/4 oz mushrooms, sliced
1 onion, thinly sliced
1 clove garlic, crushed
1 tablespoon ground paprika
$^1/_2$ cup/125 mL/4 fl oz white wine
2 tablespoons tomato paste (purée)
$1^1/_4$ cups/315 g/10 oz sour cream
1 tablespoon chopped fresh parsley or
1 teaspoon dried parsley flakes
freshly ground black pepper

1 Cook pasta in boiling water in a large saucepan following packet directions. Drain, set aside and keep warm.

2 To make sauce, melt butter in a saucepan over a medium heat, add mushrooms, onion and garlic and cook, stirring occasionally, for 5 minutes or until onions and mushrooms are soft.

3 Stir in paprika, wine and tomato paste (purée), bring to simmering and simmer for 5 minutes. Remove pan from heat, stir in sour cream and parsley and cook over a low heat for 3-4 minutes or until heated through. Season to taste with black pepper. Spoon sauce over pasta and serve immediately.

Crests with Mushrooms

Serves 4

INDEX

STOCKISTS

The publisher thanks the following companies who generously supplied props for this book.

Country Form
625 South Dowling St, Surry Hills, Sydney
Ph: (02) 9360 6299

Domus Ceramics
499 Crown St, Surry Hills, Sydney
Ph: (02) 9698 1755

Gosford Quarries
300 Johnston St, Annandale, Sydney
Ph: (02) 9810 7555

Plumes Gift Agency
100 Harris St, Pyrmont, Sydney
Ph: (02) 9552 3939

Primex Products
2/66 O'Riordan St, Alexandria, Sydney
Ph: (02) 9317 2511